Contemporary Islam

*Merryl Wyn Davies* series editor

## Who Needs an Islamic State?

Also by Abdelwahab El-Affendi

*Turabi's Revolution: Islam and Power in Sudan*

# Who Needs an Islamic State?

*Abdelwahab El-Affendi*

*Grey Seal* London

First published 1991 by *Grey Seal Books*
28 Burgoyne Road, London N4 1AD, England

**British Library Cataloguing in Publication**
El-Affendi, Abdelwahab
Who needs an Islamic state? -
(Contemporary Islam)
1. Politics. Role of Islam
I. Title  II. Series
297.1977
ISBN 1-85640-022-0

**The author.** Educated as a philosopher and political scientist, Abdelwahab El-Affendi began his writing career on the Khartoum daily *al-Sahafa*. While still young he trained as a pilot and dusted crops on the plains of Sudan. He has taught philosophy and edited *Arabia, the Islamic World Review*. He has written articles on philosophy, literature and politics for a wide range of publications in Britain, France, the U.S., Sudan and the Gulf. Dr El-Affendi is currently working in London as a diplomat in the Sudanese foreign service.

*For Eiman*

# Contents

# Introduction

THE PROBLEM with the current discourse on the political aspects of Islam has consistently been the divide between clarity of thinking and sincere emotion when this important issue is addressed. Sincere Muslims are too cautious when reviewing Muslim political heritage and tend to treat it as sacred, while the sober analysis of that heritage is usually undertaken only by non-Muslim academics or by anti-Islamic elements seeking to discredit Islam. Such condemnation has, in turn, generated ferocious Muslim reactions which sought to defend the whole of our heritage-- the good, the bad and the ugly--an approach that by necessity lapses into apologetics and confusion.

It has become absolutely necessary now to put an end to this vicious cycle of confusion and emotional traps. Muslims must now undertake on their own account a critical reassessment of our Islamic heritage which does not abandon the absolute commitment to the ideals that shaped it, but at the same time does not imprison itself within its shortcomings nor treat these shortcomings as sacred.

This work is a modest attempt to open up the debate. It attempts to combine the virtues of the critical outlook, which has hitherto been the preserve of the opponents of Islam, with a firm commitment to the Islamic ideal. It also seeks to present the major elements of the debate in a style accessible to all, which pre-supposes that the Muslim point of view will be presented in terms intelligible to Muslims and non-Muslims alike. The arguments are designed to be convincing to, and by consequence open to refutation from, non-Muslims as well as Muslims. It therefore links the debate on the Islamic state to the other contemporary debate on the nature of the modern state.

My point of departure is what I call 'the Khaldunian paradox'. The fourteenth-century Muslim thinker Ibn Khaldun addressed the problem of tension between ideal and reality in Muslim political life and attempted to resolve the issue by adopting that realism which has become the hallmark of the modern mind. He subjugated the ideal to reality and right to might simply by announcing that the Muslim ideal of the Righteous Caliphate was unattainable in our imperfect world. We have, therefore, to be satisfied with what we can get. What is attainable should be sought not in the commands of the Prophet or the actions of super-human individuals, but in the iron laws of social life which allow ideals to be implemented only if they are backed by adequate force. The science of history is the science of how to acquire and manipulate power in order to approximate the ideal demands of our ethical system which the limits posed by the logic of power permit. This idea of Machiavelli and Hobbes, which is at the core of most modern political thinking, is the negation of the Islamic point of view that seeks to subordinate the reality to the ideal. This work traces the development of this idea and attempts to present the alternative Muslim viewpoint. It sketches the development of traditional Muslim political thought to the contemporary debates on Islam and the state and on Islam and international order.

How Muslims should govern themselves has been debated for fourteen centuries, the modern debate on the nature of the state has continued for about five centuries, and Muslims have spent the last century trying to reconcile

2

Islam with the modern international order. One is aware of the difficulties inherent in the rather ambitious, not to say impossible, task of offering a brief survey of all three debates, and a critical assessment of some of their more salient conclusions, especially if one also tries to offer a personal perspective on the issues involved. If this work does not achieve its objectives in a satisfactory manner, my hope and excuse are that its shortcomings will provoke others to criticize, refute or complement it, to the benefit of all thinking Muslims and, in the end, of all humankind.

This work has not been written solely for the benefit of Muslims. It is time that we Muslims realize that we live in a global community, and that our ideas and beliefs are under scrutiny from the whole of humanity. When we think or write, we must bear in mind our fellow humans on this crowded planet. Without sacrificing our Islamic specificity, we must consider the shared premises of the current global culture, which we do from a perspective of opposition.

The Muslim self-assumed role as the conscience of humanity dictates that we clearly spell out our beliefs in a language intelligible to the whole human race. This role has been enhanced by the collapse of communism, which failed in its attempt to assume that role in the past. The Muslim voice is now the only dissenting voice in a fast homogenizing world. However, the communist demise, which stemmed from internal hypocrisy, has important lessons for Muslims. With no communist tyrannies, Muslims occupy the bottom point on the scale of democratic freedom and respect for human dignity.

Muslim claims that Islam is an education to mankind are, with justice, a laughing matter, which is why we Muslims must be harshly critical of ourselves and our history. I have been unsparing in my criticisms of all these aspects of the Muslim condition, hoping to shock many into serious rethinking. My fear is not of being proved wrong, but of not evoking a dialogue ferocious and serious enough.

3

# 1

# The Problem

## The Emergence of the Modern State

THE MAIN PROBLEM posed for Muslims by the modern state stems from its essentially amoral nature. The modern polity is an association based on expedience, and recognizes no fixed or eternal norms. Harry Eckstein captured this aspect of the modern state when he wrote that the

> State was a functional response to the general disruption of once integral society....In place of accustomed norms and princely powers that still were integral to society came pseudotheological, pseudorational metaphysics and the Idea of the sovereign State as the higher principle of society 'liberated' from convention....The sense of uniqueness and separateness engendered by the State reflects the disintegration and disjunction of social life and the attendant loss of a sense of divine or natural order. In the anomic, godless unnatural world of modernity in the making, the State was necessary, and its Idea a needed, if somewhat pathetic, fiction.[1]

What is wrong with this situation is

> The lack of a sense of wholeness in contemporary developed States. In the pre-modern polity that sense was supplied by God, by the idea of Empire, by a belief in natural order. All of

4

these can be considered majestic words for convention--for normative society. Now we have nothing left that is majestic but the State.[2]

The modern state was thus built on this normless vacuum, and proceeded to create its own norms, its own 'reasons of state', considerations that were to override all moral precepts. Men were first grouped together not according to principle but to self-interest. Then they were to be governed by the collective self-interest of the new organization which they had created. Muslims woke up from centuries of stagnation to find themselves resident within so-called national states, and were condemned forever to serve these strange creatures and worship them in place of God. 'My country right or wrong' and 'my nation *über alles*': that was the creed of the day. One no longer had to praise the Lord, or fight in His cause. It was no longer God who was the greater, but one's country, and it was for one's country that one had to kill (and be killed). It is no wonder that Muslims were plagued by chronic disorientation.


## From Ibn Khaldun to Hobbes


The term 'reason of state' reminds instantly of Machiavelli who gave politics a bad name, if only for calling things by their names and reminding princes that they were really fighting each other for power and not for the lofty principles they frequently cited. However, the dubious honour of pointing men down this road belongs (ironically in our case) to the Muslim thinker Ibn Khaldun (d. 808/1406). Ibn Khaldun attempted to do what modern social scientists claim to be doing: establish a 'science of man'. While most earlier philosophers and theorists took for granted the moral dimension of man, Ibn Khaldun wanted to strip him of this dimension and expose his 'real' motives.

This attempt to go beyond phenomena to their underlying truth has been the continuing objective of science, culminating in Marxism which claimed to have stripped man to the bone and revealed all. His essence was found to reside in his material motives, and the rest was just a veneer. Ordinary man, with his ethics, religion, emotions, thoughts, loves and hates, was nothing. He was the shell to be penetrated and transcended. In the course of several decades of Marxist experimentation, this 'shell' had been trampled upon, tortured, hanged, sent to labour camps, machine gunned and re-educated, all in search of that elusive real essence which never seemed to emerge.

Ibn Khaldun's guilt was of a different order. He discovered that people were ill-treated in the name of all sorts of ideals, and he attempted to locate the underlying reason for this state of affairs. He found it in 'natural' causes ('social', as modern scientists would say), relating to the social order. Human society, based on the extended family or clan, tended towards the creation of social units based on *asabiyya* (clan solidarity). Asabiyya is the bond that holds social groups together and is the basis of political authority.[3] Political authority in turn is necessary for the orderly conduct of human affairs and has to be assumed by the most powerful individual or group in society. Formal political authority or the state (*mulk*) is different from informal leadership (*riyasa*) in that it involves coercion and is on a higher level. Thus we find a regular pattern in human relations in which individuals tend to aggregate into groups based on kinship, following a tribal leader who happens to be the most powerful because his clan is the most prestigious and influential. This in turn leads to the formation of a state in which coercive political power is held by the leader of the most powerful kin-based group. Then follows the expansion of the state by the inclusion or subjugation of other groups and states. Finally, the state faces natural decay and collapse and is replaced by a younger, more vigorous state, normally initiated by groups of nomad origin.

The role of religion and morality is subsidiary to this pattern. Religion and morality could either corrode or reinforce asabiyya, which remains the ultimate determinant of the fate of political power. Ibn Khaldun refutes the classical argument presented by Muslim theologians and philosophers which sees religion as the basis of social order and statehood, by pointing out that history showed that most people do not seem to recognize any divinely-inspired message, but still maintain prosperous states.[4] States grow naturally out of the social order, because without a central and unchallenged authority society would be destroyed by incessant infighting. The most primitive and basic form of statehood is natural rule (*mulk tabii*), which is based on brute force. At a higher level is political or rational rule (*mulk siyassi*), which is based on the rational quest for public interest and comprises two subdivisions: where the ruler is concerned mainly with how to hold onto power and works for the public interest only in so far as it is to his advantage, and where the ruler is genuinely concerned about public welfare. The third category of government is *khilafa*, or rule based on divinely revealed law, and its main objective is to attain the happiness of people in this world as well as in the hereafter.[5]

Ibn Khaldun's stance on the role and place of religious motives in the state suffers from ambivalence at times. At one level he argues that even prophets cannot achieve success without asabiyya. For any call to be widely heeded one needs the backing of force, of which asabiyya is the only source. All those reformers who believe that the moral worth of a cause is in itself a sufficient factor in gaining a following for it are grossly mistaken, as seen from the sorry fate of numerous individuals who have opposed the injustice of incumbent rulers without securing sufficient backing.[6] However, he also recognizes a role for religion in buttressing states. For example, he says that a state can be imposed on the bedouins only through religious persuasion, since they are difficult to subjugate otherwise. However, if a religious leadership (of a prophet or saint) were to be accepted by them, it would temper their wild and competitive nature, thereby promoting mutual cooperation and deference to authority.[7] Similarly, great states emerge only as a result of a religious call or under the influence of a just cause, because the establishment of such a state requires stronger unity in the face of the superior force of rival states. Such unity could only be supplied by religion, which binds hearts together and directs the group towards a single aim. The strength of asabiyya is therefore greatly reinforced as a result.[8] Even here, however, we find the Machiavellian streak quite clear in Ibn Khaldun's thinking. Religion and the moral worth of a just cause are not the real power, but only a reinforcement of the strength generated by asabiyya.

The problem with Ibn Khaldun's reasoning becomes clear at this point. Starting from the assumption that one wants to find the universal laws of human social relations without being hampered by moral assumptions which obscure 'scientific' thinking, one ends by deriving clear moral (or immoral?) conclusions. After explaining the origins of political power, Ibn Khaldun ends by simply declaring that might is right: attempts to resist might in the name of truth and right are futile, for truth cannot in itself generate and create a rival force. This pessimism about human nature justified the attitude of resignation in the face of the decadence and rampant injustice which reigned in the Muslim world at the time, because it insisted on endless compromises with the existing powers, and did not offer any hope in transcending them.

Ibn Khaldun's ideas did not become known in the West until much later, but similar thoughts emerged in the works of Niccolo Machiavelli (1469-1527) who, like Ibn Khaldun, was a practising politician of long standing. Like his predecessor, Machiavelli operated on the principle that the quest for power created its own rules, which were sometimes outside conventional morality and religion.[9] He therefore attempted to develop a science (or art) of statecraft, outlining what the practising statesman needed to know (and do) for a successful career. Although the tactics he prescribed struck many as too callous and morally repulsive, Machiavelli did no more than draw on contemporary and historical practice in illustrating his prescriptions. All he did was to judge the effectiveness of the tactics employed 'objectively' in relation to the aims they attempted to achieve. The depravity of his prescriptions thus sprang not only from the depravity of the world he lived in and depicted, but also from his making explicit the maxim that animated that world, but was deemed better left unsaid: the quest for power at any price, and for its own sake. Machiavelli's contribution was thus merely to make his colleagues aware of what they were really doing, and advise them on how best to go about it. However, he (like Ibn Khaldun before him and most social scientists thereafter) unwittingly endorsed the depraved reality he experienced by the very act of using its maxims as the basis of his system. He implied that the decadence he described was inherent in human nature, and could not therefore be transcended. His counsel was on the best way to live and operate within its confines.

The same line of thought was further elaborated by Thomas Hobbes (1588-1679) who, in common with his two predecessors, also lived in turbulent times and was concerned primarily with stability. Like Ibn Khaldun, Hobbes held that power had its own logic, because every man's desire for power over others was practically insatiable. He deduced from this the thesis that order had to be imposed on men by a superior authority to which they all had to agree to surrender unconditionally.[10]

Again, for Hobbes the superior authority was its own justification. Not only did it reject the superiority of divine law, but it was to subject all institutions (including religion) to itself: it would thus monopolize the setting down of religious doctrine and the interpretation of natural law. Although Hobbes was prepared to allow the power of the sovereign to be limited by natural law (or the law of God, the two terms are interchangeable here), this proviso was made vacuous by the claim that the sovereign was the ultimate judge of what reason dictated and what constituted the law of nature. The sovereign was also the ultimate authority regarding the law of God.[11]

## The Liberal Reaction

It is ironic that Hobbes, by his very attempt to glorify and justify absolutism, has heralded its demise. Absolutism, which was justified only by its claims to avert anarchy, has raised many questions about the nature of political authority. By demystifying the state and stripping it of the support of any divine legitimation or higher moral precepts, he laid it, and his theory, open to attack from several quarters.

The first and most devastating onslaught came from history and contemporary political developments. Hobbes was not oblivious to the examples of Athens and Rome which had governments that were not absolute, although he condemned as misguided appeals to those models, and actually counselled banning books which referred to them.[12] Even as he wrote, however, people were experimenting with forms of government which would refute his theory. One critic of Hobbes, his fellow countryman and contemporary John Locke (1632-1704) had the benefit of hindsight when he rejected Hobbes's theory in his *Two Treatises of Government* (1690). He was writing only two years after the successful 1688 revolution managed to put constitutional restrictions on the absolute authority of the monarchy. He was thus able to assert with confidence that anarchy was not the only alternative to absolutism.

Locke made a two-pronged attack on Hobbes's theses. First, he found some flaws in Hobbes's characterization of the state of nature as one of absolute anarchy and unbridled injustice, for Hobbes was indeed mistaken to portray pre-state life as one of utter anarchy. Pre-state tribal order may be imperfect, but not to the degree portrayed by Hobbes. Many would indeed prefer a stateless communal existence to life under tyranny. And this was the second point of Locke's critique of Hobbes. He indicated that the sovereign authority of the state could be much more harmful than pre-state injustices if it were based on unbridled tyranny. He therefore proposed the idea of limited government based on the consent of the ruled.

The idea of limited government was also inherent in Hobbes's own theses. First, Hobbes himself recognized necessary limitations on the authority of the state in certain areas, such as private property, the family and personal life. Indeed, his very claim that absolute authority was necessary to counter anarchy admitted that such authority should be limited precisely to the public domain, where unrestrained individual actions could create friction. However, where individual action did not pose a threat to the state or others, what then was the rationale of putting limits on it?

Locke's theory expanded on this element, asserting that society, the community of people formed from the law of nature, was the basis and justification of the state. The state should serve the ends of society, and not vice versa. Unrestrained governments had a tendency to create ruling cliques which used the state to further their own private ends as opposed to the general interest of the community. Political authority must therefore be restrained by the division of powers (the legislative and executive powers should not be given to one organ), and by mechanisms which ensured that the government was accountable to the people.

Locke thus used a major premise of Hobbes (namely that the state was a device created by men to serve certain definite ends) to reach diametrically opposite conclusions. While Hobbes argued that the state authority should be absolute, undivided, irrevocable and unchallenged, Locke insisted that these powers must be limited, divided, revocable and open to challenge. Hobbes rejected as anathema the idea of rebellion against tyranny, even in the name of God and natural law. Since there were bound to be divergent interpretations of the divine will and the law of nature, asserting the right of rebellion was tantamount to licensing the very anarchy the state was supposed to prevent. In case of competing claims and interpretations of natural law, therefore, there is no option but to accept the interpretation authorized by the state. For Locke, by conrast, rebellion against tyranny was not only a right but a duty. If the state was there to serve society, tyrannical government was the antithesis of this institution and a great disservice to society, which could not be justified by the state's original purpose.

It is significant that while Hobbes treated the question of the state from the point of view of escaping anarchy, the perspective introduced by Locke into the argument looks at the matter from the opposite side. Locke was more concerned with combating tyranny and protecting the individual and his rights in the face of state-instigated oppression. His ideas

> Helped to inaugurate one of the most central tenets of European liberalism; that is, that the state exists to safeguard the rights and liberties of citizens who are ultimately the best judges of their own interests; and that accordingly the state must be restricted in scope and constrained in practice in order to ensure the maximum possible freedom of every citizen.[13]

This perspective was developed further by the utilitarianist
school of the British philosopher Jeremy Bentham (1784-
1832) and his disciple John Stuart Mill (1806-73). For this
school, the liberties and rights of the individual were sacred.
It was therefore absolutely vital to safeguard them by
reducing interference by the state to the minimum needed to
safeguard public order and prevent harm to others. The
authority of government should be limited by the division of
powers, periodic elections, free press and free associations.
The government must exercise its authority according to
fixed principles, central to which is the pursuit of the public
good defined as the greatest happiness of the greatest
number.

There is an inherent contradiction in these claims and
demands. While J.S. Mill was adamant that interference
with individual liberty could only be justified to avert harm
to others, the demand for the promotion of the greatest
happiness of the greatest number could justify interference
with individual liberties for purposes other than defence
against harm. These contradictions were to come to
prominence and play a central role in the rise of Marxism.


## *Hegel to Marx*


The line of thinking set off by Ibn Khaldun raised one major
problem that is still bedevilling social science. By
purporting to draw a line of demarcation between descriptive and normative theory and advocating the latter, it
courted two major defects. First, it consistently smuggled
normative content into the description of reality through the
back door. Simply by asserting that some ideals were
unattainable in reality, descriptive theory condemned these
ideals and implied their rejection. By insisting that might
was the basis of all political authority, and by discounting
the mobilizing potential of just causes in a universe

13

dominated by power considerations, Ibn Khaldun condemned humanity to perpetual incarceration within this amoral world. Similarly, by asserting the futility of rebellion against tyranny and posing anarchy and tyranny as the stark alternatives between which humanity had to choose, Hobbes was actually counselling perpetual submission to tyranny.

Second, at another level this kind of theorizing on the amoral aspects of the world soon slips into regarding the world as essentially amoral and devoid of value. Such an attitude can easily encourage immorality. It is not for nothing that 'Machiavellianism' denoted the bad name of politics, for that is the only possible politics in the world described by these scientists.

It was in Georg Wilhelm Friedrich Hegel (1770-1831) that this aspect of Western political thought came to a head. Hegel drew the necessary conclusions from the Hobbesian postulation of a state without moral constraints and saw the state as the ultimate moral principle, the locus of 'universal insight and will', the result of the unfolding of the Spirit as history: God incarnate. While Hobbes decreed that we must accept the sovereign as the ultimate arbiter in moral matters, and the French philosopher Jean-Jacques Rousseau (1712-78) sought bedrock moral certainty in the 'supreme direction of the general will' (or informed public opinion, to put it more modestly), Hegel went a bit further. Not only was the state the judge of what was right, it was the embodiment of what was right; not only was it the voice of God, it was God. Since God, the Spirit, revealed Himself in history, and the state is the end of history, then the state was the ultimate embodiment of Reason and right. Like all other aspects of history, it acquired its legitimacy from its existence. 'What is rational is actual, and what is actual is rational'.[14] In other words, might is right and things could never have been otherwise or better.

It was at this point that Karl Marx (1818-83) departed

14

from Hegel by 'inverting' him, as he claimed, while preserving the essence of his theory. Marx accepted two theses from Hegel: the idea that the world formed an organic unity, and the idea that reality had its own logic and could not be changed according to the human will. However, he differed from Hegel in his valuations. Thus while Hegel accepted that all that was real was rational (i.e., acceptable), Marx held up another aspect of Hegel's logic, the dialectic, which claimed that all that was real contained within itself its very negation, and was therefore transient. He also disputed the primacy given by Hegel to the spiritual within the organic unity of his system, and although preserving that unity, held that the spiritual was causally and ethically subordinate to the material. Thought was the creation of man's material conditions, and not the reverse.

Not only thought, but all social and political institutions were conditioned by the economic organization of society. The state, as part of the superstructure, reflected the division of society into classes, and the domination of political structure by the economically dominant class. In our time, the capitalist mode of production conditions the state, which looks after the interests of the capitalist class. The state has admittedly a limited room for manoeuvre, but all its actions must ultimately serve the interests of the dominant class. The state does not, as Hegel claimed, embody the universal will, but the class interests of the bourgeoisie.

Nevertheless, this situation, like all preceding arrangements, carries within it the elements of its very negation. The capitalist system produces the dispossessed proletariat, the unpropertied working class who have no stake in the capitalist order, and who become poorer as the system develops. This process will ultimately lead to the collapse of the system, but not before the system has created the foundations for the ultimate and just society: the communist society. The capitalist system has created the means to achieve abundance, and in fact only perpetuates itself by creating artificial scarcity. However, with the destruction of capitalism and the advent of the rule of the proletariat, there will be no need to create scarcity, and a classless society will be possible because need will be banished. And so will exploitation.

Over the last century Marx's ideas have served as the basis of some bold experiments in social engineering, which have since proved to be unsuccessful. However, even before environmentalist howls started to remind the world that scarcity will be with us for some time to come, it became clear that the collapse of capitalism was neither inevitable nor, if it were to occur, would it lead necessarily to a just, classless society. Over the years Marxism was subjected to numerous modifications to accomodate some recalcitrant facts, such as the durability of the capitalist order, the aversion of the working classes to communism and the emergence of communist bureaucracies in Easter Europe. The culmination of this process was, of course Mikhail Gorbachev's *perestroika*. The process was long, however, reflecting itself in such developments as social democracy, Eurocommunism and the New Left.

## Pluralism and the Eclipse of Ideology

The trend of thought we have been tracing here culminated in the German philosopher and sociologist, Max Weber (1864-1920). Weber tried to restrict himself as much as possible to the 'scientific' examination of the workings of the modern state. He tackled the issue of class differen-tiation, but without the passion of Marx, and tried to define the essence of the modern state, but with much less involvement than writers such as Hobbes or Mill. The modern state for Weber was 'a human community that (successfully) claims the *monopoly of the legitimate use of physical force* within a given territory' (emphasis in original).[15] This definition does not dispense completely with value content, but it shifts it to the subject matter. Legitimate force is therefore what is considered legitimate by those concerned, no matter on what basis. However, Weber does not hide his bias towards the modern state, with its formal-legal legitimation and its super-efficient bureaucracy. He rejected the Marxist critique of the bourgeois state and suggested that the abolition of private property and business organization would lead to more power concentrated in the hands of the state bureaucracy and probably irreversible tyranny. This analysis was vindicated by the experience of Eastern European and other communist and totalitarian states in the pre-Gorbachev era. Even in the era of perestroika, though, it took a tyrant in the shape of former KGB chief Gorbachev to reverse the progress towards unchallengeable tyranny.

The ideas of Weber and the experiences of Western European democracies were the origin of the various schools of pluralism and neo-pluralism, which reflected a confluence between Marxist and liberal thought. Like Marx, the pluralists recognized that Western society was not the community of equal individuals idealized by liberal theory, but was divided according to class and other criteria. Following Weber, however, they affirmed that class divisions were not as central as Marx had claimed. Other cleavages, such as race, creed, nation, etc., appeared to cut across class lines. Competition among different groups is adjudged by the state, which attempts to balance competing interests. The result is 'polyarchy', the rule of the many.

Although pluralists attempted to make explicit the positivist content which had characterized sociological theory since Ibn Khaldun, their attempts to divorce reality from value were not entirely successful. We find that their description of the modern Western democracies as governed by the balance of power between numerous competing interest groups is not completely value-neutral, for it was

17

coupled by a broad consensus among pluralist theorists which held that this state of affairs was both inevitable and beneficial. However, the problems which beset liberal democracies from the late 1960s have since sobered some pluralists a little. They have tended thereafter to emphasize that not only did liberal democracies fail to treat all individuals equally, but they also gave a raw deal to weak groups. Neo-pluralists came close to neo-Marxists in stressing the commitment of the liberal democratic state to the interests of powerful business groups, a fact which has a strong influence on decision-making and the distribution of power within the state.

## The State as a Problem

Modern political theory has turned its back on God precisely by limiting the choices open to man. The divergent accounts of how and why the state functions as it does have in common at least one central assumption: that man is not free to be perfect. State theories since Ibn Khaldun agree in discarding the idealized concept of man as a creature tending naturally towards virtue. This view which sent political philosophers since Plato in search of the perfect society perfectly ruled by a virtuous man or clique has been severely shaken by Ibn Khaldun's assumptions about self-interested ethnic groups imprisoned within the unforgiving logic of power. Anyone attempting to run the affairs of society must not be guided solely by ideals, whether heavenly or earthly, but primarily by the realities of power politics, which afford the most virtuous of reformers only a limited margin of manoeuvre. Virtue is what the logic of power permits.

While Machiavelli reaffirmed the demands of the logic of power in a humbler fashion, Hobbes postulated self-interested man, with his 'perpetual and restlesse desire of

Power after Power that ceaseth onely in Death',[16] as the basis of his system. Such an individual incessantly sought to subjugate other men and things to his desires, which was why the relations of men were based on conflict. This 'possessive individualism'[17] is at the basis of liberal theory up to Mill. Rival theories such as Marxism and pluralism, do not contradict this basic assumption about self-interested man, but view self-interested man (just as Ibn Khaldun did) as a member of a group. The self-interested group (class, interest group, etc.) replaces the individual as the main player in the game.

This principle not only rejects the idea of the collective responsibility of the human community for the spiritual well-being of its individual members, but even their material and worldly welfare. The principle of the welfare state, which is coming to dominate the world scene, attempts to do this on a partial basis and in a limited sense. It does so by default, however, and not on principle. That is why Reaganomics and Thatcherism found it so easy to roll back the frontiers of the welfare state, and triggered an avalanche that is sweeping away the relics of this principle even in communist states. The welfare state was a bribe paid to the disadvantaged to stem the tide of communism. Even then its implementation has been profoundly individualist in nature. It has shifted the duty of caring for the disadvantaged to the impersonal state, which administers the system through impersonal rules and regulations. It is not the collectivity that cares, but a machine, a 'safety net'.

For Muslims, acceptance of this model implied serious problems. The *umma* was based on the principle of shared concern for the worldly and spiritual welfare of all. Theirs was a unity of destiny, not of convenience and shifting interests. More seriously still, the Muslims found this alien model seductive. The success achieved by the 'godless' modern state was phenomenal, and it was due in no small part to its amoral and godless basis. When one builds

19

institutions on the assumption that man is basically without scruples and that rulers are generally scoundrels and potential tyrants, then one has protected society from their shortcomings. If not, then their virtues are a bonus which causes the system to function even better.

Whatever one might think of the moral basis of Western political systems, they still show a definite superiority over most political systems in the Muslim world. They are even a decisive improvement on most earlier systems of rule in Islam, barring the Righteous Caliphate and its approximations in later history. This realization, which struck early Muslim reformers such as Sayyid Jamal ad-Din al-Afghani and Muhammad Abduh, was the cause of tormented soul-searching among the Muslims. Faced with the tyranny and despotism which reigned in the Muslim world on the eve of modernity, Muslims experienced the anguish of comparing their condition to the evidently superior fairness and equity of Western systems. Neither eulogies of our great past, nor the dwelling on the undeniable shortcomings of Western democracies could hide the fact that the first destination to which persecuted Muslims flee when hounded by 'Muslim' regimes is usually a Western European capital.

It is time that Muslims faced up to this fact. The challenge is this: the Western state has been based on dubious moral and factual assumptions, but is still the most successful model around. The Muslim faith has shown a capacity to create a political order which was in many ways superior to the Western model, a superiority enhanced by the gap in time between the two experiments. However, modern Muslims have been unable to progress towards either model. Why?

That is the question.

# The Tradition

## Political Authority in Islamic History

THE QUESTION of state authority confronted the Muslims directly only after the death of the Prophet. The political structure which the Prophet established was unique in history. Unlike conventional state authority which derives much of its validity from being almost inescapable, the political authority which the Prophet established was a voluntary association. Not only was membership voluntary, but it also entailed great personal risks. Participation in the public domain (like joining military expeditions or the payment of dues) was also voluntary. The state had no method for enforcing this participation. In fact, one of the sanctions against those of dubious loyalty was precisely to deny them a share in public duties. The Prophet was instructed to refuse *zakah* (alms) payments from certain reluctant donors, and also to bar those who refused to participate in certain difficult missions from joining any subsequent expedition.[1] These sanctions were entirely moral, and bear no relation to conventional methods of state coercion.

The judicial functions of the Prophetic state were also based on morality, rather than on coercion. It was stated in the Quran that a man could be adjudged a true believer only if he accepted the Prophet as the ultimate arbiter in any dispute with his fellow believers.[2] Although this provision was enshrined in the document known as the 'Medina Constitution' (*sahifat al-Madina*),[3] the Quran stated that non-Muslims could appeal to the judiciary functions of the Medina state only if they wished to do so. Even if they did, the Prophet could choose to decline to arbitrate in their disputes.[4]

A rather different situation materialized following the death of the Prophet. With no leader of his stature to arbitrate in the numerous disputes that arose, a coercive political authority seemed indispensable. There was first a disagreement about who should become the leader of the community and on what basis. Once this matter was resolved, there was disagreement about what authority this new leader should have. While the question of leadership was swiftly resolved and with reasonable unanimity, the other issues led to civil war.

### Khilafa: Succession to Whom?

The institution of khilafa, which owes its origins to this early experiment, has stirred controversy ever since. The first question it provided was who could stand in for the Prophet once he had departed from this world. The answer supplied by those who had elected Abu Bakr as *khalifa* (successor) to the Prophet was that the best man in the community should be chosen. This thesis was immediately rejected by the rebels who refused to pay zakah to Abu Bakr. It was an important issue, since zakah according to Islamic belief was not a tax. The word means 'purification', and the payment of zakah was a religious act of purification. It had to be distributed by the Prophet or his agent, first to satisfy the needs of the poor within the locality where it was collected, and then to help the poor in other areas. It could also be used to finance some communal needs, such as supplying fighters in holy wars, building mosques, and so forth.

It was thus not incompatible with Islamic law for a tribe or a locality to organize its own institutions for zakah collection and distribution, as long as the quranic rules in this regard were observed. Two problems, however, led to controversy in such a course of action. First, those who rebelled against Abu Bakr were not rival religious leaders, but bedouin tribes whose allegiance to Islam was tenuous at best. Their view was seen as inspired by pure self-interest and lack of faith rather than by a different but sincere interpretation of the Quran. Second, this attitude appeared to the early generation of Muslims to threaten the unity of the Muslim umma which they cherished so much. If the community were to break up into small isolated units, they believed, it would soon lapse into pre-Islamic rivalry and self-destruction.

A paramount influence in the whole episode was, however, Abu Bakr's perception of his role as successor to the Prophet. Leading companions of the Prophet, including the usually hardline Omar, advised Abu Bakr against picking up a fight against the zakah rebels. Abu Bakr, however, was adamant and angrily accused Omar of cowardice, saying that if the rebels refused to hand over a tiny piece of rope which they used to deliver to the Prophet, 'I will fight them until they deliver it or I perish'.[5] The key here was a specific perception of what would have been acceptable to the Prophet. Abu Bakr viewed himself as a guardian of the Prophetic heritage, and he was in no mood to see the norms established by the Prophet tampered with.

This vision was heartily embraced by the nascent community, which found in Abu Bakr's leadership a reassurance of the continuity of the age of the Prophet. The momentum supplied by the deep commitment to the ideals of the divine message was sufficient to make this formula work in the early years. Nevertheless, from the beginning there was a universal realization that Abu Bakr was not the

Prophet. In the first statement he made after his election, Abu Bakr told his fellow Muslims:

> I have been appointed as your leader whilst I am not the best man among you....I am following [the norms established by the Prophet] and not establishing new practices. So if I get it right help me, and if I go astray redirect me.[6]

These words amounted to the constitution of the new state, being a clear indication of the character of the novel situation faced by the Muslims. In the time of the Prophet there was no question of guiding the leader, or watching out for his errors in order to correct them. God took care of that, while the community had only to follow the divine guidance. Now this guidance had to be mediated by human agents who were supposed to determine what conformed to the dictates of true faith and what did not. Who are these human agents? Presumably it was not the khalifa himself, for he was the one asking for guidance. However, Abu Bakr did not accept the opinion of those who refused zakah payment, nor the advice of those who counselled moderation in dealing with them. Apparently the khalifa accepted his conscience as the ultimate guide for his actions. Close and trusted advisers such as Omar and Ali were regularly consulted on most matters. The congregation of the Prophet's mosque in Medina acted as an informal parliament which was informed about new policies first hand and was free to debate them. However, the central concept governing that polity was that the khalifa was the privileged interpreter of the faith and a virtual successor to the Prophet, fulfilling all his public functions, including that of guiding the community.

This vision was further reinforced by the firm and unyielding leadership of Omar, who succeeded Abu Bakr as khalifa. His strong leadership was undisputed because he was harsher on himself than he was on his subordinates, and he stuck meticulously to the highest norms prescribed by Islam in both the private and public aspects of his life. He was, so to speak, an embodiment of the law, a living demonstration of how sharia, the law, was supposed to function. To oppose Omar would have literally been to oppose the law, for he would enjoin nothing else.

This tour de force, in which Omar attempted to rise to the standards set up by the Prophet and followed by Abu Bakr, obscured the fact that the status of the Prophet could not be matched by that of any successor. This realization was soon to dawn on the community with the accession of Othman to power after Omar's murder at the hands of a disgruntled non-Muslim subject. Othman's accession highlighted many problems which were left unresolved by the khilafa institution. One example was the lack of agreement on how to select the leader. While Abu Bakr's election as khalifa occurred only after a dispute in which nascent rival Muslim groups claimed the prerogative of choosing the leader, Omar's succession was very smooth. He was nominated by Abu Bakr during his lifetime and accepted without opposition. When he was stabbed, Omar nominated six candidates who were to choose the leader from among themselves. This they did only after a fierce struggle. Of the two leading candidates, Othman narrowly won, since he appeared to be slightly more popular than Ali. However, those who chose him soon came to regret it because opposition to his rule developed among many sections of the community, finally leading to a coup in which rebels occupied Medina and besieged Othman to force him to step down. When he refused, some overzealous rebels assassinated him.

This tragic episode threw the whole community into disarray. A system which was based on the ruler being a stand-in for the Prophet was not designed to cope with a khalifa whose conduct did not rise to the Prophetic standard, and its people were confused about how to deal with him.

However, the community was not prepared to see the khalifa assassinated either. The loss was double. The khalifa who was supposed to be a symbol was found wanting, and the community, who were supposed to be the guardians of righteousness, assassinated their venerable and ageing leader.

The conflict which ensued caused the community to slip even further from the ideals it set for itself, and to lapse into more desperation and cynicism. The camp of the 'idealists' led by Ali contained many of the rebels who rose against Othman in the name of this very same idealism, and was therefore tainted by the tragic assassination of the khalifa. The rival camp, led by Muawiya, made much capital out of this fact, but was by its own reckoning and by the near-universal belief of Muslims far removed from any ideals. However, Muawiya's group was well organized and clear about its objectives, while the idealists were torn apart by the anguish they felt at every compromise they were forced to make with reality. It is ironic that Muawiya's leadership was virtually undisputed in his camp, though none of his followers regarded him as remotely resembling a saint. On the other hand, Ali, who was acknowledged by most Muslims as the closest thing Islam had to sainthood, faced an uphill battle in trying to impose his authority on his followers. He encountered frequent rebellions in the name of the very idealism on which his camp was based, while Muawiya, who laid claim to no idealism, was quite safe from such demands.

## The Power-State

The inevitable result of these tensions was the collapse of the idealist project and the relapse of the Muslim community into pessimism and despair following the triumph of the Machiavellian state which we have seen Ibn

Khaldun later trying to justify. Muslim thinkers did not see the root of this collapse in the self-contradictions of the original vision which attempted to assign the role of the Prophet to ordinary men. They instead tried to find comfort in the belief that following the death of the Prophet, the world had entered into a spiral of inevitable decline which would only be arrested on the eve of the Day of Judgment. This relieved the Muslims from the duty of trying to look for a way out of this impasse and shifted the burden on to the inevitable laws of history. The political fortunes of the Muslim community confirmed this pessimism as they descended from the heights of the Righteous Caliphate to the abyss of factionalism and despotism that only ended in the collapse of the Ottoman Empire following World War I. Then followed the even darker times of Western colonialism.

The Righteous Caliphate was a period when the tension between the ideals of the Muslims and the reality of their lives was minimal. The rulers consistently and conscientiously sought to adhere to the law in letter and spirit, and the community were largely in agreement on most matters, including the interpretation of the law. The prosperity of the community and their self-esteem were increasing, and all seemed to find fulfilment in communal and political life. With the schism that developed in the last years of Othman's rule, this peace with the self was shattered, never to be regained.

When the dust settled over the momentous struggles unleashed by the murder of Othman in 36/656, the Muslims found themselves under the despotic regime of Muawiya (41-60/661-80). The Umayyad state was not recognized as legitimate by most Muslims, but only tolerated. It faced numerous revolts until it finally collapsed following the triumph of the Abbasid revolution in 132/750. The Abbasids soon fell short of the expectations of Muslim idealists who fought the Umayyads in the hope that their fall would herald the return of the Righteous Caliphate. Shi'i and Khawarij revolutionaries therefore continued to challenge the Abbasid state.

Nevertheless, with all its shortcomings, the early period of the Abbasid era was to be mourned as a golden age when the regime lapsed into the brutal military dictatorships of the Turkish commanders favoured by Caliphs after the days of al-Mutasim (d. 227/842). These commanders gained virtual supremacy after the murder of al-Mutwakkil in 247/860. The collapse of caliphal authority and the fragmentation of the state which followed turned the office of the Caliph into a popular symbol, reminding the masses of the golden era when the unchallenged authority of the Caliph could be appealed to for justice and reassurance. From then on the Muslims suffered calamity after calamity: the Crusades, the Mongol invasions, Memluke tyrannies, and so forth. This continued until the pax Ottomanica intervened from the sixteenth century onwards to restore some calm and order to the troubled Muslim realm.

The harking back to the early golden age of the khilafa was not a purely romantic projection, but referred to some objective characteristics which distinguished that era from the succeeding periods of chaos and despotism. While Muslims were confident that the power of the Caliph, the Islamic law and the consensus of the umma more or less coincided during the Righteous Caliphate, the Umayyad and the early Abbasid eras were also periods during which the influence of the community and their values were still a potent force. Caliphs went to great lengths to court the approval of the ulema and other dignitaries, and were careful not to be seen contradicting the letter of the law. The decay of the political system was thus characterized by a progressive decline in the role of the wider community in political affairs, further reinforcing the pessimism at the basis of Muslim political theory.

28

## The Development of Muslim Constitutional Practice

The various ideas about the nature of political authority in Islam evolved gradually from reflections over early political practice. The first principles enunciated by Abu Bakr stated that (a) the Arabs would only defer to Quraish; and (b) that obedience to the ruler was due only in so far as he obeyed God and His Messenger. Implied in this was the belief that the community were judges of whether the khalifa really followed the commands of God and the Prophet, which meant that ultimate authority rested with the community. Abu Bakr, as we have seen, also believed that he represented the authority of the Prophet. This implied that despite the theoretical authority of the community, ultimate political authority rested in practice with one person. This was confirmed by Abu Bakr's rejection of the suggestion by the Ansar of a shared authority between two leaders, one from Quraish and the other from Ansar.

Later on, Abu Bakr found it expedient to designate a successor in order to avoid the recurrence of the confusion following the Prophet's death. Omar later followed suit. However, a new problem arose when Othman appeared to have lost the confidence of the community, but refused to step down, claiming that the privilege of being Caliph could not be taken away or abdicated. All these ad hoc decisions were later regarded as precedents with normative significance.

When a theory of the khilafa started to crystallize in later periods, it was built on these early precedents. The essence of that theory was first to assert that the establishment of the khilafa is mandatory (citing the consensus of the early generation as direct evidence, and quranic and Prophetic allusions as indirect evidence); it has to reside in one person (it can neither be a collective, nor can there be multiple rulers); this individual has to be the best, most virtuous and most competent male Muslim from Qurashite lineage; he has to be designated by the influential leaders of the community (*ahl al-Hal wa'l-'aqd*); and he has to observe sharia but cannot be replaced or disobeyed even if he commits flagrant transgressions.

The bitter experiences of internecine conflict which led to the collapse of the Righteous Caliphate also caused Muslims to realize the futility of violence. While the two rival camps faced each other, each claiming to be the sole guardian of Truth and Right, both were soon ready to compromise their positions to achieve peace. Muawiya said he would be happy to serve under Ali if the latter handed over the alleged killers of Othman, while Ali later accepted arbitration; his son al-Hassan struck a deal with Muawiya, legitimizing the latter's rule on certain conditions (that al-Hassan succeed him after his death). All these compromises were struck only after horrific bloodshed and destruction, which caused most thinkers to counsel against violence for resolving political disputes. They outlined minimum requirements for legitimate rule, and stressed that law-abiding rulers should not be opposed by force. Even when a ruler's behaviour was below standard, an uprising was advisable only if its chances of success were very high. This position led to a spiral of concessions and was later to be used to legitimize almost any kind of rule.

The expected reaction to this defeatist stance soon occurred. The tiny rebel groups known as *al-Khawarij* (the rebels) had emerged during the war between Muawiya and Ali. When Ali accepted arbitration following the inconclusive battle of Siffin (37/648), these men split with him, alleging that accepting arbitration was tantamount to giving men a say in a matter already resolved by God. Later they even accused all their opponents of abandoning Islam. Their doctrine forbade any compromise whatsoever, and all those who opposed their view were to be fought to the bitter end. The fanatic idealism of al-Khawarij soon provoked external and even internal conflict, for they themselves disagreed over the content of the divine commands they were fighting to enforce. This phenomenon was surprisingly enduring, however, and the determination and zeal of these groups became legendary.

Between these two poles of defeatism and fanaticism numerous positions emerged. Most notable was that of the Shi'a (party) of Ali. In its inception the Shi'a position was a broad political stance which favoured Ali as a leader over Muawiya, not because of who he was but because of what he stood for. The instability of the party was caused by the differing opinions of myriad splinter groups on the party programme. Later, members were narrowed down to those who supported the community leadership of Ali and his descendants. This position was apparently in response to the establishment of the hereditary principle by Muawiya, since Ali's party was originally opposed in theory to hereditary office. Anger against Othman, who was criticized for allegedly appointing too many of his Umayyad relatives to key positions in the state, was a major cause for the revolt which ended his rule and brought Ali to power. Ali himself declined to nominate his son as successor, although he did not object to his being freely elected by the Muslims. (Omar, it should be recalled, objected categorically to the appointment of any of his relatives to key positions, either during his lifetime or after his death.)

The principle of heredity did not resolve the matter for the Shi'a any more than it did for their opponents. At least three different lines of succession competed for the allegiance of the Shi'a. Over the years the Shi'a developed from a mere political party to a fully-fledged sect, diverging from the mainstream in several areas of law. However, the successes achieved by Shi'a-inspired states did not lead to a divergence from the general practice of the power-state established by Muawiya, with its reliance on coercion, illegal taxation and corrupt dispensation of public funds. At one point in the fourth century AH almost the entire Muslim

World was under Shi'i rule. However, none of the states which emerged as a result diverged in any significant way from their rival Sunni states. Some were even more iniquitous and further removed from the ideals of Islam than the decadent neighbouring or earlier states.

## Idealism and 'Secularism' in Classical Theory

In spite of all these misfortunes, Muslim theory stubbornly refused to compromise with the status quo, although it was unable to come to grips with it either. Up to the time of Ibn Khaldun, Muslim thinkers insisted on just outlining the ideals to be fulfilled by the Caliph and continued to regard any contravention of these ideals as a sin which could only be tolerated in case of extreme necessity. Classical Islamic political theory, therefore, remained revolutionary in essence even though it appeared to accommodate the realities of power politics and justify the status quo. The regimes of usurpation were justified only through necessity, which meant that they were tolerable, but not legitimate, and only as long as they could not be removed.

It is important to note that traditional Muslim political theory was first developed within the Shi'i movement during its pre-sectarian phase. That was because all authoritative leaders of Muslim opinion tended to join the idealist camp led by Ali, or else to adopt a neutral posture while not hiding their sympathy with Ali. After Muawiya's victory, leading Muslim thinkers continued to support the rebels who defied despotic political authority in the name of Islamic ideals. If the two main Shi'i schools challenged the existing order on principle, the four main Sunni schools were equally critical. Abu Hanifa (d. 150/767), founder of the Hanifa school, was persecuted by Abbasid Caliphs for suspected sympathy with Zaidi rebels and for his refusal to take office within the Abbasid regime. Malik ibn Anas (d.

179/795) was also harassed by the Abbasids for allegedly assuring rebels that their pledge of allegiance to the Caliph was invalid because it was taken under coercion. Muhammad ibn Idris al-Shafi'i (d. 204/819) narrowly escaped execution for his alleged involvement in a rebellion. The resistance of Ahmad ibn Hanbal (d. 241/855) to the attempts by al-Mamoun to impose a particular doctrine regarding the nature of the Quran caused him much suffering, but finally led to the triumph of his point of view.

The actual experience of the Muslim community, however, forced these thinkers and their successors to adopt a more realistic attitude. In the end, a broad agreement evolved among classical Muslim writers about several issues. They accepted that all regimes since Muawiya did not reflect the ideals of Islam and thus could not be accepted as a model. Such regimes were tolerable only because the alternative was anarchy and civil war. If a way could be found to replace these regimes without too much bloodshed, then their removal would be a religious duty. Although this could be construed as a vindication of the attitude of the khawarij and other rebels, it is ironic that the futile exploits of the khawarij only reinforced the belief that rebellion was inadvisable, and was not to be considered as a realistic option.

As a result of this attitude a schism developed in the Muslim psyche. While Muslims rejected secularism in principle, they adopted it in practice. A central aspect of the unitary Muslim vision of the state was that the state interacted with the rest of Muslim life. Not only did the state submit to sharia as interpreted by the community, but it also enriched and redefined sharia and the spiritual life of the community. The acts of the Prophet as a statesman and a warrior, as well as those of his lieutenants, appointees and 'righteous' successors were regarded as examples and an indication of what was lawful. However, with the rejection of the legitimacy of the state in later periods, the community stubbornly refused to accept state interference in 'spiritual' matters, or to accord it moral authority in Muslim affairs. People submitted their bodies to it, so to speak, but never their souls. The ulema gave counsel that was not much different from that ascribed to Jesus: 'render unto Caesar that which is Caesar's'. So Muslims were instructed to obey the rulers, but only where their orders did not lead to sin. However, sin was here narrowly defined, with the usurpation of power and the unlawful disposition of the wealth of the Muslim community seen as no grave sin. What is this if not secularism?

## Problems with the Classical Theory

In its later 'realistic' phase, Muslim political theory faced and created many problems. Based on the practice of the Righteous Caliphate it had nevertheless to deal with a different reality, that of the power-state. Its attitude to this reality was coloured by two contradictory sets of aspirations. First, it was concerned that the example set by the Prophet and the Righteous Caliphs must remain the guide and the standard against which all practice was to be measured. But, second, it also realized that diverging interpretations of what that model implied could, and did, lead to costly conflicts which all righteous Muslims should do their best to avoid. Muslims therefore argued that if, despite their carefully laid down provisions, a usurper were to take power by force, without being qualified or designated in the appropriate manner, then although his rule was not strictly speaking lawful, caution should be exercised in resisting him. An imaginary index was stipulated within which the usurper's deviation from the 'Righteous' standard was weighed against the cost of removing him. If the ruler undertook to respect sharia and outwardly conformed to Islamic norms, then his regime should be considered formally legal, and it must be obeyed, even if it committed grave contraventions of the sharia unless, that is, his removal could be secured at a reasonable cost.

Thus, the theory attempted to reconcile the revolutionary content inherent in recognizing only the Righteous Caliphate as a model with the equally idealist concern for minimizing suffering and disruption of the community's peaceful existence. Taken literally, however, the theory offers little guidance on Muslim rule if the bottom line is that whoever takes power is a legitimate ruler. This is especially so with later theoreticians such as al-Mawardi and al-Ghazali, who insisted that despotic rule not only had to be tolerated, but must also be accepted as legitimate. Failing that, Muslim social and religious life would collapse into lawlessness. Thus this theory had the interesting consequence of allowing the legitimacy of the whole Islamic edifice to hang on subjective decisions regarding how far an individual ruler deviated from orthodoxy, and how difficult it was to remove him.

The theory had another weakness in that not only did the theoreticians take the practices of the Righteous Caliphs as the standard norm against which all political practice was to be measured, but later writers even regarded some acts of Umayyad and Abbasid Caliphs as normative. The justification for this claim was that their acts were performed in the presence of learned ulema and companions of the Prophet who could have opposed them if they were unlawful.[7]

However, it should have been clear from the start that the deeds of the Righteous Caliphs, let alone the despots who succeeded them, could not be on the same level as those of the Prophet. Even the standard set by the Prophet's actions could not be taken out of context. One could not conclude that sending military expeditions against foreign powers was lawful or mandatory simply because the Prophet once authorized such expeditions. One should enquire about the circumstances, reasons, moral justifications, the principles involved and so forth. Regarding all acts of the Righteous Caliphs as normative could beg the question. It also led to numerous absurd conclusions. For example, al-Mawardi cites Abu Bakr's appointment of Omar to succeed him as proof that it was perfectly legitimate for any ruler to choose his successor. He neglects the fact that such an act was considered valid not only because an individual decreed it, but also because it was approved by leading Muslims at the time. He overlooks, too, the significant difference between Abu Bakr's nomination of Omar and Muawiya's imposition through brute force of his son as successor. These are gross inadequacies in any theory.

The debate on political authority was plagued by many other problems from early on, particularly the insistence on expressing opinions in normative terms, thus camouflaging the key political questions as theological arguments. The status of the person who commits a grave sin, an issue which is at the root of the divergence of the schools of Islamic thought, was primarily a political question. It was raised by the khawarij, who accused their opponents of abandoning Islam by deviating so much from its norms. Their opponents in the mainstream claimed that although the accused may have sinned, he still remained a Muslim. A middle position was adopted by the rationalists (later known as al-Mutazila), who asserted that the person who committed a grave sin was neither a Muslim nor a non-Muslim, but occupied a position in between.

The duties and qualifications of the ruler were also couched in idealist language. The erroneous identification of the ruler as a replacement of the Prophet rather than a mere official answerable to the community created confusion and unrealistic demands. The ruler was required to be pious, courageous, learned and virtuous. Since such a person was extremely rare, any ruler was by definition unsuitable, and therefore illegitimate. Because these idealistic formulations were used to justify situations that were farthest removed from the standards set by the Prophet, a serious and increasing gap was created between the ideal and reality. Had the theory concentrated on the practical functions of the government in a given state, then it would have been much easier to formulate a constitution to which the ruler would be required to adhere. However, by setting unattainable standards, it was easy to pass from the conclusion that perfection was impossible to the claim that all imperfect situations were equal. The present 'imperfect' situation was therefore the best possible situation.

It comes as no surprise then that this theory had contributed directly to the practical decline of the umma. As it stood, its major influence was to discourage reform, because it counselled against principled resistance to tyranny without suggesting a viable alternative. Moreover, its advice against resorting to force applied only to the pious who did not want to cause unnecessary mass suffering to the umma. However, the pious would in any case try to observe Islamic morality and did not need this guidance. By contrast, tyrants would not heed pious advice anyway. Since Abd al-Malik told a Meccan congregation at the start of his rule that 'anyone who after today says to me, "be conscious of God," I will have him beheaded', Muslim rulers made it abundantly clear that they did not want to hear any advice which conflicted with the 'reason of state'. On the other hand, classical theory did not offer any recommendation on how to deal with such tyrants and dislodge them, which was the kind of guidance the pious needed, not advice about the limit to which they should tolerate tyranny. The classical theory was thus at once superfluous and inadequate.

## Lessons from the Past

We must, of course, recognize that the traditional Muslim

polity could be adjudged as defective only in a relative way. It was deficient in relation to its own ideals as defined by the example of the polity created by the Prophet and perpetuated for a short period after that. Looked at from another angle, however, the Muslim polity continued to be markedly superior to any other contemporary state-form. One has only to compare the horrors suffered by Egypt during the brief Napoleonic occupation to see how well-governed in comparison were both Memluke Egypt, which Napoleon disturbed, and the Egypt of Muhammad Ali's regime which succeeded that of Napoleon. Yet both these forms are viewed as two of the worst Muslim regimes on record.

It is also interesting to note that the periods which the Muslims regarded with horror as periods of darkness and usurpation were characterized by undeniable advances, especially in the area of institutionalization. They were times when rulers concentrated on dealing with the realities of life as it was, and accepted the frailties of human nature. They refrained from pushing the community too hard, and were content to legislate for ordinary men, rather than saints. Thus we have seen the standardization of the quranic script in Othman's time, and further amendments to it in the time of the notorious al-Hajjaj ibn Yousuf, whose reign also witnessed the first Muslim coinage, the tightening-up of conscription rules in the army, the arabization of the *diwan* (the register) and many similar reforms.

It was no coincidence that the followers of al-Shafi'i were to preponderate among theoreticians in the political field,[8] for it was al-Shafi'i who pioneered the standardization of legal theory. He insisted that the authenticated Sunna of the Prophet be the basis of Islamic law rather than the fluid, regionally diverse 'consensus' of the Muslim community, presumed to be based on Sunna, because this fluidity assumes that men are inherently perfect and tend towards the right conduct. However, just as an orally transmitted Quran would have suffered corruption, or at least significant variations, had it not been committed to writing, so the practices of different communities were likely to be affected by many factors which could not all be beneficial.

Unfortunately, the formalization and standardization affected the mere form of khilafa theory rather than its content. Even when laid down as law, this theory assumed saintly perfection in men (especially rulers, who are normally the farthest removed from sainthood). This is in part a reflection of the abiding Shi'i attitude which influenced this theory from its origins and affected it in the course of polemics with the Shi'i opponents of the mainstream. The Shi'a insisted that the imam (or leader), who was the deputy Prophet, had to be as pious and infallible as the latter had been. So the Sunnis agreed that the ruler must be the most pious Muslim around (although some later Shi'is, in particular the Zaidis, agreed that a ruler could be someone who was not necessarily the most virtuous individual, and were followed in this by some Sunni thinkers). Here is precisely the problem. Qualities such as piety and virtue are difficult to ascertain objectively. Additionally, the insistence on perfection in the khalifa has automatically removed from the community the right to criticize him, for everyone is by definition less pious, less learned and less wise than he is. In the end, the fate of the umma hung on the arrival of an individual who would unite in his personal charisma, saintliness and power. The waiting for this impossible arrival was bound to relegate Muslim thinking to the realm of mythology and passive ineptitude.

In the end, a major defect in classical theory was that it was at once too idealistic and too pessimistic. In its essence it was revolutionary, setting the highest standards and urging Muslims to transcend imperfect reality towards them. Yet, it also contained the belief that these standards were unattainable and it was futile to pursue them. To escape from this impasse, the theory needs to be revised by detailing the ideals inherent in Islamic history and norms in a more realistic fashion, and then insisting that they be adhered to. A moral exhortation demanding the impossible is an exhortation to immorality. We must explain the requirements of Islamic morality in politics in practical terms, and then accept no excuse when practice does not measure up to these demands.

# The Modern Debate on the Islamic State

THE CURRENT DEBATE on Islam and the state first flared up with the outbreak of the Kemalist revolution in Turkey following Turkey's defeat in World War I. The apparent collapse of the khalifa's authority following defeat and occupation led to much anguish among Muslims world-wide. The issue was of particular concern in India, provoking a serious debate and leading to the formation of the Khilafat movement in 1919. In Turkey itself the question was raised when the Ottoman Sultan-Caliph attempted to use his religiously-sanctioned authority to suppress the rival regime set up by the Kemalist revolutionaries in Anatolia. He obtained from Shehul-Islam a fatwa which branded the rebels as outlaws who should be fought in the name of Islam. The Kemalists responded by ridiculing the Islamic creden-tials of a ruler who was in fact captive in the hands of the British occupying Istanbul at the time. The sympathies of the whole Muslim world were with the Kemalists, not with the Caliph. The latter's defeatist stance discredited the office and made it much easier for the Kemalists to take him up later.[1]

Once the Kemalists achieved victory, they took up the issue again. In November 1922 the Grand National Assembly voted after heated discussions to set up a purely spiritual Caliphate with no political authority. In

justification of this decision, Mustafa Kemal delivered a
lengthy speech in which he tried to find support for this
position in Islamic history.[2] He claimed that the institution
of the Caliphate proved unworkable from very early on
because 'one individual, however virtuous and capable,
could not administer a whole state'. He added that Omar
himself realized this, and that is why he did not appoint one
successor but a 'consultative council' of six men to assume
the burden.

The Ottoman Empire which assumed the Caliphate in
923 AH, Mustafa Kemal continued, soon began to decline.
However, the Turkish people who had set up that state had
now assumed their own affairs, and eliminated those
'extravagant' and 'corrupt' individuals who burdened it
with their ambitions. Real authority had now returned to the
people. As for the Caliphate, it is going to survive beside
popular authority in the same way it had survived for
centuries in the Abbasid era as nominal authority beside the
real authority of the Sultans. In fact, the new Caliphate
would be even more dignified, since it would have the
backing of the whole Turkish state. The new prosperous
Turkey would become the rallying point for all Muslims.

Similar arguments were put forward in a book produced
by the Grand National Assembly in 1923 under the title *The
Caliphate and National Sovereignty*. The book started by
distinguishing between two types of Caliphate: 'real' and
'nominal'. The first is where the khalifa had been freely
chosen by the community which had real power, was competent and fulfilled all the conditions laid down in Islamic
law. All other types of Caliphate were purely nominal. The
book then went on to say that it was no longer possible to
have a real Caliphate, since one important condition, that the
khalifa should be from the Prophet's tribe of Quraish, could
not be met. Muslims would not be contradicting sharia,
therefore, if they were to establish a normal government not
headed by a khalifa, given the impossibility of finding one.

The Caliphate was not an end in itself, but a means to an end, which is the achievement of justice and the preservation of the nation. The classical theses about the obligatory nature of the Caliphate merely referred to the fact that the umma must have a government which should establish justice and apply the law. An organization could take care of this as well as an individual leader. In fact, the ulema had long accepted this when they approved of nominal Caliphs who reigned while real power resided with other officials.

## The Islamist Reaction

The theses of the Kemalists did not go unchallenged in the Muslim world. At first there was universal jubilation at the bold moves taken by the revolutionaries to revive the institution of the Caliphate by appealing to original Islamic principles and enlightened rethinking. Many telegrams were sent to the Grand National Assembly congratulating it on 'reviving the Righteous Caliphate'.[3] However, as the real intentions of the Kemalists in abolishing the Caliphate became clear, the mood within the Muslim world changed.

Some voices had been raised earlier, contesting some of the arguments put forward by the more zealous Kemalists. Most notable was the voice of Rahsid Rida editor of *al-Manar*, who followed the Kemalist revolution with cautious endorsement at first, but with more outspoken criticism later. Rida first sided with the revolutionaries, rejecting the claims of the Sultan to represent Islam while his government 'was captive to the enemies who occupied its capital' and forced it to accept 'the disgraceful peace treaty which usurped its independence and dismembered its territory'. The Kemalists, on the other hand, had 'rejected this humiliation and fought it with the force of arms, winning the sympathy of the whole Muslim world'.[4]

Even when Mustafa Kemal delivered his speech on the

Caliphate, Rida maintained his cautious support. He rejected Kemal's claim that the khilafa was contrary to the interests of the nation, and refuted his argument which sought to justify the new system by reference to past Muslim failures. For Rida, the existence in the past of nominal Caliphs whose powers were usurped by military commanders did not vindicate the adage 'might is right', as the Kemalists attempted to prove. He admitted that the Kemalists' influence and the sympathy they had generated in the Muslim world stemmed mainly from their military prowess and their victories against the enemies of Islam, but this did not legitimize anything and everything these officers cared to do.[5] The situation in Ankara was abnormal, Rida argued on another occasion, since the country was run by a military government. Matters could only be settled when peace returned and the people had their say.[6]

After the publication of *The Caliphate and National Sovereignty*, Rida's criticism grew more severe. He rejected as heretical and unorthodox the claim that the khilafa was not a religious institution. He also condemned the introduction of the categories of 'nominal' and 'real' Caliphate as foreign to Muslim orthodoxy. Muslims distinguished only between legitimate rule and rule by usurpation. Mainstream Muslim thought also recognized that the degree of legitimacy of any rule varied according to how closely it approached the ideals set up by the Prophetic model. Therefore the argument that all forms of rule which succeeded the Righteous Caliphate were illegitimate was invalid; nor could it be used as a justification for the abandonment of Islamic rule altogether. Past injustice and unbelief was no excuse for current malpractice. Rida also refuted the Kemalists' claim that a khalifa hailing from Quraish could not be found today, and pointed to several worthy candidates. He also strongly rejected the argument that the khilafa was a means to an end (just government), and therefore could be replaced by any other form capable of attaining that end. The same argument, he said, could be used to replace sharia by any other code, by saying that the aim of sharia is to achieve justice, and therefore any just code would suffice. One could even say that since the main purpose of religion is to purify the soul through worship, then any religion which was conducive to this end would do, and it need not be Islam.[7]

## *The Abd al-Raziq Controversy*

The events in Istanbul provoked a wider discussion in the whole Muslim world. In India the Khilafat movement agitated for the restoration of the Caliphate, and contributed some theoretical input to the debate, such as Abul-Kalam Azad's work on the Caliphate, which was serialized in *al-Manar* starting in 1922. The publisher of *al-Manar* himself contributed a series of articles which were later published in book form as *al-Khilafa aw al-Imama al-Uzma* (1925).

However, the opponents of the khilafa also inspired an intellectual movement of their own. Following the publication of the Grand Assembly's book, an Egyptian member of the ulema exploded a bombshell by publishing later in 1925 a work denying that the khilafa had any credible genealogy in Islamic practice entitled *al-Islam wa Usul al-Hukm*. The author was Shaikh Ali Abd al-Raziq (1887-1966), a sharia judge and a graduate of al-Azhar, and his main theses were:

1. That the Prophet did not establish any state and that his authority was purely spiritual.
2. That Islam did not prescribe any definite system of government, and that the Muslims were free to choose any form of government they saw fit.
3. That the types of government established after the Prophet's death had no basis in Islamic doctrine, and was

merely an expedient form adopted by the Arabs and dignified by the term khilafa to endow it with a religious legitimacy.

4. That this system had been the source of most of the problems which beset the Muslim world, since it was used to legitimize tyranny and impose decadence on the Muslims.

The book provoked a storm in religious circles, leading al-Azhar to strip Abd al-Raziq of his title of alim. Abd al-Raziq was indicted for deviation from classical Islamic doctrine on seven counts, most notably:

1. His claims that the Prophet fought his wars for political not religious motives.
2. His denial of the existence of any consensus among Muslims regarding the khilafa.
3. His assertion that sharia was a purely spiritual code of conduct, with no positive legal content.
4. His assertion that the state set up by Abu Bakr and his successors was irreligious, i.e., secular.

He defended himself by appealing to apparently contradictory statements in his book. For example, he referred his critics to statements that the Prophet's authority exceeded political authority. Later he tried to meet his opponents halfway by saying that if Muslims today decided that the khilafa was the appropriate system within which to conduct their political affairs, then this system by this very fact would become legitimate. He also conceded that the Righteous Caliphate was legitimate precisely because it was based on the consensus of the Muslim community. Nevertheless, even in these statements Abd al-Raziq was holding his ground by insisting that the consensus of the people was the source of legitimacy, and not the principles of sharia.[8]

Part of the controversy that Abd al-Raziq provoked was caused by the confused manner in which he presented his theses. The first of the two main arguments in his book was that the traditional khilafa system was not mandatory and was not strictly based on sharia. Muslims were therefore free to adopt alternative forms of government if they saw fit. The second point was that Islam did not prescribe any political norms whatsoever, and that Muslims were free to conduct themselves in any acceptable way in their mundane affairs. While the first argument was strongly supported by many Muslim reformers, the second was the weaker of the two and was easily refuted by Abd al-Raziq's opponents. However, the confused presentation of the arguments militated against any positive input the author might have contributed to the debate. Al-Azhar's opposition to the work also opened a controversy about the freedom of thought, since many liberals supported Abd al-Raziq even though some disagreed with his views. It followed that this episode did little to advance Muslim thought on the issues at hand, and a long period of stagnation followed. Even when Abd al-Raziq later reversed his position towards the end of his life, he did not add anything to the debate by explaining the reasons for his new position.[9]

## The Emergence of the Modern Islamist Movement

The period that followed the abolition of the khilafa in Turkey in 1924 was one of deep anguish and disorientation for Muslims. For the first time since the advent of Islam the believers were left without a central authority claiming to be the protector of the faith. As in previous troubled times, the sense of tragedy spurred many potential reformers to action.

It was in this atmosphere that the Muslim Brotherhood was formed in Egypt in 1928 by a young schoolteacher named Hassan al-Banna (1906-49). The rise of the Muslim Brotherhood coincided with the last stages of the Khilafat movement which, from its base in India, had exerted considerable influence over the rest of the Muslim world, giving rise to many conferences and meetings. The Khilafat movement aimed to revive the Caliphate; when that became impossible there were attempts to transfer the supreme Muslim office to an existing monarch or ruler. These attempts again failed because of rivalry between several competing candidates, none of whom had exceptional credentials anyway. The failure of the Khilafat movement signalled the end of an era when the existing Muslim states could still be expected to address the urgent issues facing Islam. For the first time since the Prophet assumed supreme political office in Medina in 622, Islam because a stateless religion, an ideology in search of a home. This opened an era which paved the way for mass action and seriously questioned the legitimacy of all existing rulers.

The Muslim Brotherhood and similar reform movements were thus a response to the failure not of one state, but of the totality of Muslim states in satisfying the needs of the faithful. They also reflected the influence of modernity, most notably the modern state which became not only the framework within which these movements were to act, but also their main antagonist. Earlier reformers such as Afghani could still roam the Muslim world from India to Egypt and call every town within it home. They also shifted their allegiance, hostility and advice from ruler to ruler without giving a thought to the problem of frontiers. For later activists, this became largely impossible. The Muslim Brotherhood, after some initial uncertainty, was forced to recognize that it was first and foremost an Egyptian movement, and thus confined to the reform of the Egyptian state and society.[10]

For the Brotherhood, reform had to start with the struggle for independence from colonialism, the building within independent Egypt of a strong state based on Islamic principles and the striving for prosperity and social justice on the basis of sharia. However, al-Banna did not dwell much on the character of the state he wanted to see installed, since he was more concerned with individual and social reform. He insisted that his main aim was to 'awaken the spirit and revive the hearts'. All desired reforms would then follow from this central aim.[11] Creating the Muslim individual would create the Muslim family and thus the Muslim nation.[12] The Islamic state would be the fruit of this reform programme, and not its starting point.

There were some ambiguities in the thought of al-Banna, since his theoretical denial of the primacy of the state did not prevent him from engaging in fierce political struggle, nor from repeatedly calling on governments and politicians to shoulder their responsibility to Islam. Later in his life, al-Banna appeared to have become more convinced that the role of the state in his proposed Islamic reforms was important. The fight against colonialism, the reform of education, law, the economy, etc., needed the state to act. Thus we find some of his later writings addressed more and more to 'His Excellency the Prime Minister' and to heads of societies and groups. This led al-Banna also to pay more attention to the form of government. He accepted that constitutional representative government accorded well with Islamic ideals, but the form it took in Egypt needed some amendments. In particular, he detested party politics and argued that it was divisive and served no useful function in Egypt. He also wanted electoral reform so that Parliament would include *ahl   al-Hal wal-Aqd*, the leaders of the community. In his reckoning these included competent ulema, experts in public affairs and local or prominent community leaders.[13]

The setbacks which the movement suffered because of its confused politics led to the relegation of the state to an even lower level in theory, while it became the central issue in practice. The repeated crackdowns to which the movement was subjected under the monarchy during the years 1948-50 and under the military regime of Gamal Abd al-Nasser in both 1954 and 1965 meant that the very survival of the movement depended on the attitude of the state towards it. Leading theoreticians such as Sayyid Qutb (1904-66) insisted that Muslim activists should give politics a low priority, and stick to the struggle to form a virtuous community by following in the footsteps of the Prophet. The formation of the first Islamic state was the culmination of years of spiritual formation during which the Muslims shunned all compromise of the type that characterized normal political activity. Today the Muslims must not, in the manner of conventional political parties, promise people the earth and the moon to win support for their programme. They must not even put forward a political programme, for the virtuous society they sought to create would certainly be free from most of the problems currently facing nominally Muslim societies. It was therefore a waste of time to try to solve the problems of a society that would not even be there when Islam arrived.[14]

Although the experience and attitude of the Muslim Brotherhood were not conducive to extensive discussions on the state, the Jamaat-i-Islami of Pakistan (founded in India in 1941) gave this issue much thought because of the advanced stage of Westernization in the Indian subcontinent and also because the question of a Muslim homeland was of paramount political importance for Indian Muslims. Sayyid Abul Ala al-Maududi, the founder of Jamaat-i-Islami, thus gave an early answer to this question.

After rejecting the Muslim nationalist claims that a state based on a national identity for the Muslims could lead to an Islamic state eventually, he affirmed that the Islamic state was an act of collective worship based on the principle of khilafa (vicegerency). As man is God's vicegerent (khalifa) on Earth, God is therefore the sovereign in a Muslim polity and the community are equal in the responsibility and right to administer the state. This polity could therefore be styled a 'theo-democracy', in that it is a democracy constrained by divine law.

The purpose of the Islamic state was to promote virtue and combat vice by all possible means. From this last assumption Maududi deduced that the Islamic state must be totalitarian, akin to communist or fascist states. It was also an ideological state in which men acquired citizenship solely on the basis of their beliefs and on no other consideration such as race or class. Maududi then reaffirmed the classical assumptions which required that a single individual, the most pious member of the community, must assume the khilafa. He should be assisted by a consultative council representing the community, but he was authorized to override the opinion of the majority in the council. The council and the whole community would have no right to oppose his decisions in individual cases, but could remove him if he no longer enjoyed their confidence.

To attain this state a virtuous community must first be created, for the state was merely a reflection of the social conditions within which it emerged. Therefore, a nucleus of dedicated men committed only to Islam must rise and struggle until they gained moral hegemony in society, and thereby influenced the emergence of an Islamic state. Unlike other states which were based on the subjugation of man by man (directly or through submission to manmade laws, ideas or theories) this state acknowledged only the sovereignty of God.[15]

Maududi's vision faces several problems emanating from the unsuccessful reconciliation of classical theory with modern concepts. The sovereignty of the community which he affirms is negated by allowing the khalifa to be a virtual dictator. His belief that the state must have the ultimate responsibility to promote virtue and combat vice meant necessarily that the state must be totalitarian, thus interfering in the private affairs of individuals. Another problem is created by two assumptions: that the ruler must be a pious dictator, and that the community which should control the state must be a virtuous community. Apart from the fact that virtue and piety are difficult to ascertain objectively, modern Islamist groups generally regarded themselves as precisely this virtuous community. This, coupled with a pessimism regarding the capacity of the Muslim masses for creating the desired Islamic state, created a gulf between these movements and the masses. Needless to say the condescending and arrogant attitude of the Islamist groups did not endear them to the populace, and therefore confirmed their suspicions about the public's response to the call of Islam.

For a while this attitude permeated the vision of the whole modern Islamic movement, until an opposing trend appeared in the 1960s and 1970s: the Sudanese Muslim Brotherhood led by Hassan Turabi and the Tunisian Islamic Trend Movement (ITM) of Shaikh Rashid al-Ghanoushi presented an alternative vision. Turabi, who also gave much thought to the question of the state and had much practical involvement in it, approached the issue from a method-ological angle, arguing that the state represented a central legislative principle in Islam, but so did popular consensus. Turabi rejected the traditional assumption (also held by Maududi) that authoritative consensus meant the consensus of the ulema. For him, binding consensus was that of the Muslim populace (or public opinion) at a given moment. Popular choice should be enlightened by experts, including the ulema, but also including experts in other fields, such as economics, medicine, law, the social and exact sciences, etc. Even if we look at Islamic history we find that the dominant schools of thought were selected by free popular will. The government should also be freely chosen to reflect the popular will. Once this had happened, then the elected government would have a religiously significant legislative role, and could arbitrate in differences on interpretations of sharia. Thus Turabi by one stroke elevated the state to the role of religious adjudicator and subordinated it to popular will. [16]

Al-Ghanoushi went even further by limiting the role of the modern Islamic movement to that of just another actor within the liberal-democratic state. While even Turabi seemed to regard the Islamic movement as the guardian of Islamic morality within the state, a role that Islamists have assumed since the demise of the khilafa, Ghanoushi rejected this idea. For him, the Islamic movement had neither a monopoly in the interpretation of Islam, nor in dictating morality. It was just another political party offering its programme to the people, and inviting them to decide freely between it and rivals. That this could lead to the adoption of non-Islamic programmes, given the nature of the modern national state, as Maududi predicted, did not seem to disturb him. As the movement was not a guardian of the people, all it could do was preach and attempt to persuade. What the people chose was their business.[17]

This attitude, however, assumed that democracy and freedom were maintained within the state. As yet Ghanoushi could not say who would guarantee such freedoms, and seemed at a loss when faced with a situation like that of present-day Tunisia where the movement is not allowed to campaign freely. Would the movement then fight for democracy, or would it accept permanent illegality?

## *The Iranian Revolution*

For most of the post-khilafa period, the Islamic state has been no more than an idea, and most of the movements aspiring to attain it resided in the Sunni Muslim world. For the Shi'a, who did not recognize the khilafa anyway, life went on as it had for centuries before, waiting for the Mahdi who would come from above to right all wrongs. However, the modern challenge which faced the Muslims in our age did not spare Shi'i communities either. In fact, the leading Islamic reformer of the modern era, Sayyid Jamal ad-Din al-

Afghani, was most probably of Shi'i upbringing. Afghani also co-operated with the Iranian ruler Naser al-Din Shah (1848-96) before being thrown out of Iran after disagreement with the monarch. He later played a leading role in urging Shi'i ulema to orchestrate the tobacco embargo of 1891-2 to force Naser al-Din Shah to rescind the tobacco monopoly he had granted to a British company. This show of ulema power later gave them a strong, if transient, influence during the constitutional movement of 1905-6. That constitution gave the ulema a role in scrutinizing laws to be passed by Parliament. In spite of this activism, however, Shi'ism remained devoid of a theoretical basis for positive and sustained action on the political field-- until the arrival of Ayatollah Ruhollah al-Musawi al-Khomeini.

Khomeini took the side of the burgeoning Islamic activism among the modern-educated youth in Iran, and chastised the ulema for not showing similar activism. In the course of his political and intellectual struggle against the Pahlavi regime in Iran, Khomeini managed to revolutionize Shi'i thought in an unprecedented fashion. Shi'i thought was activist in essence, and in its Zaidi version (dominant in Yemen) it still counsels perpetual rebellion against tyranny. However, the *ghaiba* (occultation) theory introduced at a later age shifted the responsibility of righting wrongs onto the absent Imam. Khomeini pointed to the contradictions between these two stances, for waiting for the Imam meant toleration of all possible evils. And since Shi'ism does not accept postponement of other religious duties (such as prayer and Hajj) and since it has become quite clear that even these can be eroded under the corrupting influence of despotic regimes, there can be no excuse for neglecting political duties.[18] Khomeini's rethinking was complemented by the input of the revolutionary thinker, Ali Shariati (d. 1977), whose powerful and explosive synthesis of traditional Shi'i thought and modern revolutionary theory had a strong appeal for Iranian youth. Shariati's ideas acted as a bridge between tradition and modernity, and made public opinion receptive to Khomeini's traditionally based revolutionary call.

In reaffirming the central role of the state in Islamic life, Khomeini also extended the authority of the interim institution fashioned by Shi'ism to oversee communal religious functions: the jurist-guardian. This institution, better known as *velayat-i-faqih*, operated in many areas of Shi'i life, such as inheritance or guardianship of orphans. Khomeini wanted the institution extended to cover politics as well. Just as competent jurists deputized for the Imam in administering social life, they should als be his deputies in running the state.

With his charisma and the allegiance he commanded from the Muslim masses, Khomeini made this deputization into something more than a mere formality. He reaffirmed the original concept about the virtuous Caliph, traditionally accepted in both Shi'i and Sunni circles and added the idea of the determinant role of the state in religious affairs. In a statement in February 1988, Khomeini affirmed that the state's interest takes precedence even over all other religious duties, because the upholding of the Islamic state is the paramount religious duty.[19] This idea resembles Turabi's concept of the state as a legislator, but it comes more naturally to Shi'i thought which sees the Imam as the infallible deputy of the Prophet, and therefore the source of paramount religious authority.

In practice, the Islamic Republic of Iran was beset with many problems, and for most Muslims, including many Shi'i Iranians, the ideal Islamic state remains just that: an ideal and a dream. For a start neither the citizens nor the rulers of this utopia appeared to be divinely-inspired saints. They were instead fallible humans, who could and did jostle with one another for power and influence, and who fought over material things as violently as did infidels, and sometimes more so. They were prone to disastrous mistakes, which does not make them much different from many illustrious early Muslim rulers of the past. In short, the Iranian experience has raised more questions than there were before about the adequacy of various versions of traditional Muslim theories of virtuous government.

One important defect in traditional Muslim political theory revealed by the Iranian experience is the inadequacy of institutional safeguards within that theory. It showed how easy it was for a small group of people to monopolize authority in the name of ideals to which they themselves did not adhere. The Iranian regime appeared to many as tyrannical, and there was no recourse for ordinary Muslims who disagreed with the rulers. Because the constitution was tailored for a ruler who was supposed to be the closest thing to an infallible imam, the question of how the government's despotic behaviour could be remedied was not adequately addressed.

The grievous sufferings to which many innocent Iranians fell victim because of the defects of some of the narrow-minded individuals who claimed to represent the authority of Islam has demonstrated amply that the first thing Muslims needed to do is to give up the idea that their rulers have to be virtuous. Modern Muslim activists have been too concerned with the establishment of the principle of Islamic rule, to the extent that they have neglected to create adequate safeguards to make this principle work. Not every one who supports the idea of Islamic government is a saint, and Islamic history is mostly a history of villains who claimed to rule in the name of God.

## Conclusion

The basic problem with the current Islamist vision of the state is that it accepts the modern concept of the state as a principle of restriction. This conflicts with the original Islamic vision of the polity as a principle of liberation and self-fulfilment. In addition, modern Islamic thought has imported into the debate all the ambiguities and confusions of classical Islamic political theory. Like their illustrious predecessors, today's Muslim thinkers appear to yearn for that elusive virtuous autocrat, a sort of Mahdi who would recreate and re-establish the Prophetic vision with divine sanction and help. This attitude is a great help to existing despots, but has yet to bring the Muslim dream nearer to realization.

Adding to the problem is the totalitarian quasi-utopian vision in which the Islamists conceived of a mighty state dragging an unwilling community along the path of virtue and obedience to the law. These Islamists have concentrated mainly on the prohibitions and restrictions in the law, so much so that many modern Islamist movements which were denied the most basic freedoms have pleaded to flagrantly non-Islamic regimes to restrict the freedoms of others, regarding this as an extension of Islamic life. A sad illustration of this tendency are the recent appeals by Islamists in the Gulf states, where the media is subjected to incredible restrictions, for controls to avert the dangers of satellite television which threatened to promote permissiveness. It seems, therefore, that the citizen these Islamic groups seek to create is essentially someone who is deprived of the freedom to sin, even if there is not the freedom to be virtuous either. This was certainly not God's purpose when He created man and woman and endowed each with free will.

4

# The Islamic State and International Order

HOBBES'S MODEL of a chaotic society characterized by constant war 'of every man against every man' was not entirely fictitious. It was based, as he himself asserted, on the international community of his time, where the absence of a central coercive authority capable of imposing order on nations meant that 'in all times, Kings and Persons of Soveraigne authority...are in...a posture of war.'[1] However, even in the international arena war does not reign indefinitely. Sooner or later, some balance of power is created which serves as the basis of an international 'order'. In the past this had been achieved by the rise of one or more powerful empires, each imposing order in its sphere of influences. Although this order was by necessity imperfect and was prone to collapse, as it did on many occasions, it would soon be re-established in some form or other.

In our time until recently, the international order had been underpinned by the demarcation of two major spheres of influence, one controlled by the Western bloc led by the United States, and the other controlled by the Soviet Union. A vague area in between gave rise to the Non-Aligned Movement (NAM) which worked more to stabilize the system than to challenge it. Since 1989, however, this system has started to collapse, following the abdication of the Soviet bloc and its near-total disintegration. The world has now temporarily become a single sphere of influence dominated by the West, but this is only a transitional system. A more durable and clearly defined 'order' has yet to take shape.

## Muslims in the International Order

The mention of Islam in the context of international relations brings to mind Iran and Lebanon. Earlier, the Qaddafi regime in Libya was also thought to reflect Islam's disruptive influence in international relations. If we add Afghanistan, these four countries have done more than any other power to turn the international order upside-down and make all the rules of the game redundant.

The phenomenon of 'disruptive Islam' indicates that the international order now in its death throes was established and stabilized in the absence of Muslim influence. In fact, it was shaped mainly at the expense of the Muslims. The Ottoman Empire, the central state of the Muslims on the eve of modernity, was mutilated and partitioned by the imperial European powers, while the quasi-totality of the Muslim world was subjugated by force to the political will of these same powers. France, Britain and Russia between them occupied and ruled most of the Muslim world, leaving a few rejects here and there to weaker states such as Holland, Spain, Portugal and Italy. By the end of World War I only three or four Muslim countries escaped direct European control, and even they were not entirely autonomous since they were still subjected to a certain degree of manipulation.

The Muslim world started to gain political independence after World War II, but it was achieved only conditionally, and within the context of the prevailing 'international order'. Thus, each Muslim state was born into a framework which it had no hand in creating, and was supposed to conform to it. A new country had to join the United Nations and sign its charter; it had to join international monetary agencies, accept international laws and conventions and subscribe to the prevailing values governing the international order. Not surprisingly, the rules tended to enshrine the dominance of the major, primarily European and Western, powers.

However, the Muslim world was unique among the emerging Third World nations in that it possessed an internal resistance to this system. Thus while many countries with long-standing non-Western traditions (such as Japan, China and India) were happy to integrate into the new world culture with varying degrees of ease, most Muslim countries appear to have stubbornly remained outside this emerging consensus. Those governments which worked hardest at integration (such as Iran, Turkey and Indonesia) could continue this uphill endeavour only by resorting to severe repression so as not to suffer a horrific backlash. Most other countries tried to maintain a balance which none seems to have achieved yet. Even here, however, regimes such as that of Pakistan, which wanted to be 'part of it' still rely heavily on enormous foreign military and economic aid to support them in this tug of war.

The integration of Muslim states within the present international order thus remains precarious, tentative and incomplete, mainly because these states have not yet found themselves. Free discussion to resolve the issue of Islam and the state has been stifled in most of these countries. It may be recalled that when Mustafa Kemal was unable to direct the debates of the Grand National Assembly the way he wanted, he banished the debate on Islam from the public arena by using brutal repression.[2] His example has since been faithfully followed by many other rulers: Bourguiba, Nasser, Suharto, to mention but a few. However, this issue stubbornly refuses to go away. The success of the Islamic revolution in Iran, coupled with the rise of powerful political and intellectual Islamist movements in Egypt, Pakistan,

Lebanon, Sudan, Jordan and elsewhere have reopened the debate. It is now the central issue facing not only the Muslims, but also the world.

The end of the Cold War has focused increasing attention on the Islamic question, first because the demise of communism left Islam as the only political creed opposed to the now internationally recognized Western political ideology, and second, the re-emergence of the Soviet Muslim republics as a political force promises to have profound implications for the international order. The Soviet Muslim republics could either separate from the Soviet Union and thus hurry the collapse of the Soviet empire or they could become influential within the USSR and thereby force at least one superpower to accommodate Islam in its agenda.

## The International Order Challenged

The rise of militant Islam in Iran and elsewhere has raised serious worries among the guardians of the present world order, who fear the role Islam is likely to play in world affairs will be subversive. But Islamic militants are not, of course, the only critics of the international framework. Earlier, the Marxists led by Lenin chastised the world order as an 'imperialist' system propelled by the logic of capitalism. The capitalist system required military expansion in search of raw materials, markets and invest-ment outlets, which in turn led to competition between rival capitalist powers for the conquest of the world. The result would be destructive wars leading to the ultimate collapse of capitalism.[3] This theory, which proved to be inaccurate, was later refined to describe the emergence and performance of multinational corporations. This development, it was argued, necessitated an imperialist ordering of the world to safeguard the interests of this type of institution, the activities of which recognized no frontiers.[4]

Other radical theorists, such as Samir Amin, Immanuel Wallerstein and André Gunder Frank, also attempted to describe the world in terms of the hegemony of world capital which gives the international order its salient characteristics.[5] These authors argue that the captalist world economy, which had started to take shape in the sixteenth century, now embraces the whole world. Individual states are defined primarily by their place within this system. They are either core states representing the heart of the system (such as the United States, Western Europe and Japan), or peripheral countries dominated and exploited by the core countries which has expanded their capitalist economy to encompass them. The core countries are characterized by advanced industrialization and the prevalence of the capitalist mode of production. The peripheral states, on the other hand, are dependent on the centre which controls their economies and extracts surplus value from them. Between these two camps are the semi-peripheral countries, less advanced and independent than core countries but more so than peripheral countries. These countries, which in Wallerstein's view include the socialist bloc, help to stabilize the system by acting as a buffer between the two strata.

One does not have to agree with either of these two views to accept that the international order is characterized by an economic stratification favouring the industrialized nations. It is important to recognize, however, that this stratification has now acquired a primarily cultural basis which is only secondarily economic. In particular, the state system operates to sustain the international order on this basis--for example, by immigration controls in the industrialized countries. The advanced countries have become more and more restrictive in admitting newcomers, and the criteria they apply are becoming more blatantly racial and cultural. At times these countries consciously sacrifice economic efficiency to safeguard dominant cultural and racial traits within their societies and to restrict the enjoyment of prosperity to certain cultural groups. The most obvious example is South African apartheid, for which the far Right in Europe does not hide its admiration. However, the divisions within the international system are different only in degree. The Third World 'homelands' are no less artificial than the bogus South African creations, or the refugee camps in occupied Palestine. Such discrimination is legitimized by international law, in which the designation 'foreigner' makes it perfectly acceptable, even patriotic.

We also see this kind of bias in the media and in the political activity of these states. Huge resources are deployed to highlight and respond to the plight of one 'American citizen' anywhere in the world, while the sufferings of whole nations may go unnoticed. The attitude to the apartheid regime in South Africa or the Palestinians in their homeland are a case in point. Hugh economic resources are deployed to uphold the perceived rights of white individuals of Western origin against millions who are neither white nor Western, sometimes (as in the case of Israel) without any conceivable economic return to those footing the bill.

## The Return of Islam

The Islamic critique of the present world order is based on different premises. Although Islam is by nature opposed to injustice and racial discrimination, and therefore bound to clash with the unjust basis of the system, this is not the primary point of divergence. The revival of Islam seems to clash with the prevailing order precisely because this order embodies the usurpation and subversion of Islamic history, and represents the nadir of the progressive decline of the Muslim umma.

As the international system par excellence, Islam concerned itself with world politics from its inception. It was the first creed to proclaim an international mission based on the equality of all people. True, ancient empires from the Assyrian through the Roman had proclaimed their aspirations towards or illusions about ruling the world, but their ideas were based on the subjugation of other peoples to a particular nation or individual. Only with Islam was the idea of a world community, unified under one political authority based on equality before the law, set forth in unprecedented clarity. Early Muslim history embodied this ideal and transformed it into a living reality. When, at a later stage the Muslim polity deviated from the ideals of the faith, one important factor which induced the early generations of Muslims to tolerate this deviation was their perception of this holistic dimension of the Islamic political order. The deficiencies in the internal order were more than compensated for by the rising prestige and achievements in the international sphere. The power-state of later ages stood condemned in the light of true Islamic values, but since it represented a marked improvement over all competitors, Muslims were rightly proud of the positive contribution it made to the world around it.

With the stabilization of the outward expansion of the Muslim polity, there was a growing awareness of the deterioration in the standard of government, as revealed by the onslaught of invading infidels (Mongols, Crusaders, etc.). Sincere Muslims were shocked to see unscrupulous princes colluding with alien infidel powers to gain and retain power. A particularly scandalous example was that of the warring princes of Muslim Spain in its age of decline which set in from the beginning of the eleventh century. By the start of the sixteenth century, the collusion of Muslim princes with the infidels became the rule rather than the exception. Treaties with Western powers consistently gave unfair advantage to the latter, and progressively undermined the independence and integrity of Muslim states. Whereas in the past the Muslim polity was forced merely to accommodate the whims of its own despots, it was now supposed to pander to the whims of the infidels as well. No wonder the Muslim polity was taxed to the extreme.

This led inevitably to colonialism and the complete loss of autonomy by Muslim states. The post-colonial international order is attempting to perpetuate the legacy of colonialism by employing the emerging élites to do its job for nothing. The new states established in the Muslim world as an integral part of the current system stifle Islam's self-expression at home; and when Islam manages to wrestle itself free in one state, the whole world assumes an actively hostile attitude. Such behaviour only enhances the conviction that this order is inherently unjust, and brings out the internationalist aspect of Islam, which attempts to remould the whole world to achieve justice and moral probity.

This aspect of Islam may be described as subversive, although the subversive nature of Islam is not political but moral. The very existence of Islam as a belief subverts the system. Political containment is impossible, for even if all the Muslims were to die tomorrow, Islam as a moral indictment of the present system would remain to haunt it. The answer to Islam has to be sought at the level of ideology, or no answer will ever be adequate. The West has occupied the whole Muslim world and ruled parts of it for many years. It still occupies Muslim Central Asia in the name of communism and internationalism. Yet all these creeds and movements have receded into history, while Islam is still going strong. The confrontation is not likely to end here.

## The Status of Non-Muslims

One curious by-product of the incorporation of the Muslims into the alien world system was to make the status of non-

Muslims within a proposed Islamic state a central issue in any discussion of political Islam. Non-Muslims, it was argued, could not have complete equality within an Islamic state, and therefore this state was intrinsically unfair and should not be created.

This argument is inherently imperialist in its basis, for Muslims also could not have full rights in a non-Islamic state. However, that was not thought to be a problem, but rather the natural thing. Indeed the issue originated in the imperial designs of the West, which attempted to undermine the Ottoman state by extracting from it the 'capitulations', which as the word implies are just that: the imposition of the rule that individuals under the protection of Western powers (normally citizens of those countries, but later even indigenous non-Muslims) were to be exempt from Islamic law. Later, with the colonial occupation, Islamic law was abolished altogether except in the 'personal' sphere, relating strictly to family matters, such as marriage, divorce and inheritance. Attempts to restore Islamic law on the eve of independence were opposed because this was prejudicial to the status of non-Muslims and therefore not to be allowed.

Islamists reacted by alleging, with reference to traditional texts and history, that Islam had always been fairer than most systems in its treatment of non-believers. Whereas in the ancient world, even in post-Muslim Spain, non-believers were given the choice between adherence to the established religion or death, Islam recognized non-believers and granted them detailed rights. Some Islamists even insisted that non-Muslims should be given full citizenship in an Islamic state, citing the Medina Constitution which granted the Jews a status of equality in the first Muslim polity. Nowadays some Islamists argue that the contract of *dhimma* (protection), according to which non-Muslims were granted protected status (regarded as *dhimmis*), has been superseded. The collapse of the Islamic state by the abolition of the Caliphate meant that one party to the contract is now absent. The re-establishment of an Islamic state must therefore be achieved on a new basis, where non-Muslims resident in its territory will be considered co-founders of this state, and therefore full citizens with equal rights to Muslims.[6]

The non-Muslims to whom these arguments were addressed were not impressed, however. For them an Islamic state, even one which enshrined their rights in its constitution, was not acceptable. This rejection was based on the allegation that non-Muslims, especially where they were in a minority, could not aspire to hold high office in an Islamic state, which therefore deprived them of an essential right.

One would indeed consider an Islamic state run by an infidel a curious institution. However, the problem goes deeper than this, for it involves the very nature of the modern nation-state and its place in the world. In order to be established at all, a state must gain international recognition, its borders must be guaranteed by international conventions against encroachments, while its survival and that of its government depend on active economic and political co-operation of influential members of the world community. A country can be starved economically or deprived of essential armaments which are needed to protect its integrity, its borders and its sovereignty within these borders.

It is clear, regardless of the particular situation of Muslim communities, that the Muslims represent a marginalized minority within the modern international order. The task of creating an Islamic state, which should include non-Muslims, has to be resolved within this system which, regardless of the proportion of non-Muslims, exacts special treatment for them. Thus a decision on the norms of governing a particular Muslim state cannot be made by its citizens without taking into account the wider international community. A non-Muslim minority can appeal to this wider community and can count on effective support to remedy perceived grievances. Muslims, by contrast, even if they are an overwhelming majority in a country, find it difficult to affirm their norms in the face of resistance from the outside world and can count on little effective support from Muslims elsewhere in such a case.

In earlier times, the traditional Muslim response to such a situation would have been to emigrate to a new territory where Muslims could set up their own community free from interference from hostile forces. The present international order, however, rules out mass migration in search of a new state. The last such attempt, the establishment of Pakistan, was not a complete success, for even here there remained a substantial non-Muslim minority to be accommodated.

## Islam and the Nation-State

From the above discussion it seems that there are indeed difficulties in reconciling the institution of the modern nation-state with Islamic principles. However, one must qualify this conclusion with several assertions.

A major source of confusion in the current discussion of the nation-state and Islam stems from basic linguistic misunderstandings. Pundits, and not only Orientalists but many distinguished Muslim writers as well, argue that Islam admits traditionally of only two concepts of international relations, namely the division of the world into *Dar al-Islam* (the abode of Islam) and *Dar al-harb* (the abode of war). However, this classification is based first on a mis-translation, and second, on an omission. The mistranslation pertains to the second term, which could be more accurately rendered 'hostile territory', for Muslims refer to Dar al-harb not only in contradistinction to Dar al-Islam, but also in opposition to *Dar al-ahd* (non-Muslim friendly territory with which there is a pact or *ahd*). Thus the expression Dar al-harb becomes eminently simple to comprehend within a commonsense formula of international relations. A territory becomes hostile not on an ideological, but on a political basis, since it is neither Muslim territory, where Islamic law is valid, nor a territory that is willing to co-exist with Muslims on the basis of a peace agreement. It is the omission of the concept of Dar al-ahd from most discussions on this issue which has created this long-lasting misunderstanding.

On the other hand, the problem for Muslims with the modern state lay less in its form than in its substance. It is not that Muslims reject the nation-state *per se*, but that they reject any polity not based on Islam. Any piece of territory governed according to Islam becomes instantly Dar al-Islam, be it a town, a country or a continent. One can say that the compatibility or incompatibility between Islam and the nation-state is mainly a pseudo-problem, for the question is less one of a particular formula for the subdivision of the world into political units than one about the actual grounds on which the division was made. The present international system has expended hugh resources in order to create and support artificial institutions with the express purpose of subverting the free self-expression of Islam in the political sphere. The conflict is thus between the substance, and not the form, of this international order and the values of Islam.

The confusion is further compounded by politically motivated arguments, exemplified by claims that Islam is 'inimical to the core idea of the state', or that Arab and Muslim states 'do not operate as Western states do', and therefore will not resolve their disputes with Israel in the same manner as disputes among Western states are settled.[7] A major flaw in this argument is of course that it omits a basic variable, namely that Israel also is not an ordinary state in the sense in which Western states are ordinary. It was neither established nor is it governed in a normal way. It is based on a religio-politial challenge to Islam. There is, therefore, nothing abnormal in the 'abnormal' Arab response to this very unusual phenomenon. Western states would probably react in even stranger ways to a similar challenge. The allied claim about foreign policy being a European concept totally 'alien and new in the world of Islam'[8] is problematic mainly because it is premised on the confused mistranslation already discussed.

There has also been endless confusion over the use or misuse of the word umma (community), also a simple non-religious term which acquires significance when joined to another term, such as *ummat-al-Islam* (the Islamic community). To say, as many commentators endlessly repeat, that a Muslim is required to render absolute allegiance to the umma and then conclude that this precludes allegiance to a particular state is a double misunderstanding. First, a Muslim is required to reserve his or her allegiance to God only. A Muslim submits to God within the community and not to the community. The community could swerve in its allegiance to God, and it is then incumbent on the true believer not to follow the herd but to strive to guide the community back to the right path. Second, within the context of absolute allegiance to God, particular institutions such as the family, the tribe, the nation and, one would add, the country, are not effaced but sublimated and given a new expression within the new context of belief. Thus, Islam recognized tribal and territorial divisions and actually institutionalized them.

The main guidelines regarding these allegiances were given in great detail with regard to the family. Believers were instructed to respect kin bonds, even when their kin were non-believers, and were urged to do good even to non-believing parents. However, they were warned not to let this compromise their faith and their duties towards the promotion and preservation of the Muslim community. A true believer was thus portrayed as someone who was immensely kind to his or her parents but unswervingly firm in resisting their inducements to abandon the faith.[9] This guideline was intended to influence the Muslim's attitude to all similar natural bonds, such as tribe, territory, locality, etc. (It is significant that Sayyid Jamal ad-Din al-Afghani referred to non-Muslim compatriots as 'our neighbours'. The category of neighbour is an important one in Islam, and the Quran urges Muslims to be extremely courteous to their neighbours.) In fact, many modern Islamists viewed current political relations in this light. Hassan al-Banna placed the modern Muslim inside several concentric and mutually reinforcing circles: the individual, the family, the nation (country), the wider nation (the Arab community) and finally the Muslim world. Hassan Turabi similarly regards the particular subdivisions into nation-states as natural and valid. Just as the family is not incorporated into society by dissolving it but by preserving and strengthening it, so individual states need not be abolished to form the Muslim world or the pan-Arab nation. They are incorporated as organic wholes into the overall formula without losing their individuality.[10]

However, rejecting as mistaken the theses of those who, like Lewis and Pipes, hope to prove that Islam is essentially incompatible with the idea of international order, does not entail subscribing to arguments such as those proposed by Hassan Turabi and Ismail Raji al-Faruqi, according to which Islam is committed to world peace and order.[11] These suggestions must be contrasted with the opinions put forward by Sayyid Qutb who, following Maududi, rejected the idea that Islam favoured peace and order. Both writers assert that Islam is a revolutionary doctrine which cannot tolerate injustice and the subjugation of man by man. Islam is a revolution against injustice and falsehood in the whole world. Its very proclamation threatens entrenched interests which resist it and try to stifle it, so the mission of Islam cannot be complete unless injustice and falsehood are uprooted from all corners of the earth. As a liberating

71

ideology Islam must attack and defeat all tyrannies which enslave man to man, no matter where they are. It cannot restrict its mission to a territory or a nation, since it is inconceivable that the universal message it proclaims would be true this side of a mountain or a river, and false on the other side. Islam, therefore, cannot wait to be attacked and then justify fighting back as 'self-defence'. It attacks unjust systems everywhere. Nor does this contradict the quranic injunction against compulsion in religious matters, for Islam does not fight people to convert them but it fights the tyrannical systems which oppress men and women, struggling to liberate them from oppression and then leaving them free to choose their beliefs.[12]

One must accept that the Roman and Persian empires conquered by Islam were not exactly liberal democracies which guaranteed the rights of man and freedom of conscience. Offensive war against those states could not therefore be said to have violated any rights, except the right of tyrants to do what they liked in their own domains. Humanity is forever under the obligation not to extend laissez-faire to protect Naziism, South African apartheid or the genocidal Khmer Rouge regime of Cambodia. However, the emergence of modern democracies where people are relatively free from direct coercion in matters of conscience has posed new questions for Muslims. Some responded with new, bold suggestions. The leader of the Tunisian ITM movement, Rashid al-Ghanoushi, uses the traditional definition of Dar al-Islam as the land in which Muslims are 'free and secure', and where they can practise their religion publicly without fear, to deduce that Western democracies have become, for all practical purposes, part of Dar al-Islam. Muslims should forget about hostilities against these countries and concentrate on peaceful interaction with their peoples. Since these places are now open for peaceful propagation of the Islamic faith, the stage in which Muslims had to fight to get their message across is gone forever.[13]

For a long time this has been the unspoken assumption guiding the foreign policy of modern Muslim countries, which seem to have accepted the general idea of peaceful interaction as the basis of the modern international order. However, this does not justify the conclusion reached by Majid Khadduri that Islam has now 'completely reconciled' itself to the present Western-inspired international order.[14] Such statements were consistent with the prevailing attitude of writers in the 1960s, who were keen to announce the death of political Islam,[15] a statement which represents a 'gross exaggeration', to paraphrase Mark Twain.

The proponents of those ideas have lived to see their mistake. It is now generally recognized that Islam is going to be a significant factor shaping tomorrow's international relations. The role of Islam as the sole remaining major challenger to the liberal-democratic Western-dominated international system has indeed been enhanced by the demise of communism. This has placed a grave responsibility on the shoulders of the Islamic nations, which must first put their houses in order and then see that justice and equity rule in the international order. Therefore, the Muslim world must undergo a prolonged period of internal change before it can assume its international role.

# 5

# Beyond Resignation and Fanaticism

## The State for the Muslims

THE MODERN ERA has confronted Muslims with conditions that are in many ways radically new. They were the product of earlier human responses to circumstances which confronted people in the past, and include guidance on appropriate reactions. In dealing with these conditions, Muslims faced, and still face, immense difficulties. Being a Muslim did, of course, dictate that the response to these conditions must be governed by Islamic principles, but the difficulties surrounding attempts to act Islamically in the political sphere go back much further than the modern era, and have exercised Muslim thought for centuries. The modern era only helped to highlight certain strands of traditional political thought, in particular the realist and pragmatist tendencies represented by such writers as Ibn Khaldun.

### Reality and Its Laws

It is true that the modern experience of the Muslims, to say nothing of earlier periods, has impressed on all concerned the absolute necessity of paying more attention to the worldly reality to which the religious morality is supposed to apply. Particularly in politics, one ought to examine

74

closely the relevant factual (social and natural) laws to determine how best to bring this sphere in line with the ideals and norms dictated by Islam. However, there is the danger of a tendency to regard the regularities discovered in the social sphere as immutable, and thus to neglect the fact that the social space is essentially the sphere of action of the human will. Social scientists since Ibn Khaldun have apparently subscribed to a double fallacy. They regarded social laws as god-like forces which governed reality, while at the same time negating any role for the human will in shaping or modifying these laws.

This fallacy inevitably led to numerous self-contradictions. Ibn Khaldun appeared to vacillate between considering asabiyya to be a sovereign force under which all other influences in politics were subsumed and regarding religion as essential for the efficacy of asabiyya, especially for the creation of states. Hobbes suggested that self-interest ruled supreme in the social sphere, limiting the choices open, but called for measures to stabilize society which presupposed the existence of many options. Marx outlined all sorts of 'iron laws' governing human behaviour, but saw typical acts of unconstrained human will, such as the 'heroic' struggle of the working class and its allies including deserters from other hostile classes, as an integral feature of the social field. Without such acts of the will the social laws would not function as they were 'supposed' to do.

In the end, all these theories fail because they neglect some essential facts pertaining to the regularities they describe, and minimize the impact of certain aspects of reality. Ibn Khaldun believed that the ability of people to transcend the confines of the self-interested kinship groups towards a more universal human community was such a rare occurrence as to be discounted as irrelevant. Hobbes underestimated the ability of people to cast aside narrow self-interest in favour of fruitful mutual co-operation. Marx's theory was destroyed by its failure to take account of human creativity in the social and technological spheres, a factor which has enabled the capitalist state to transform itself into the welfare state and thus avoid starving the proletariat into revolution. It also enabled capitalism to escape the iron law of declining returns by continual technical innovations, and thus falsify Marx's predictions about the collapse of capitalism because of this factor.

The lesson for Muslims is an important one. The search for the laws governing reality must not be a recipe for submission to those laws in place of God, nor an invitation to cynicism and amoral resignation. We cannot shout after Hegel that 'all that is actual is rational' and then go to sleep. We cannot even believe with Marx that although reality is not what it should be, its very laws are going to bring us salvation whether we like it or not. It is essential to believe in the unlimited capability of the human will to strive for perfection. In the past people have proved themselves capable not only of defying social laws, but also of creating and abolishing them. The history of Islam is the most eloquent proof of this immense human potential.

Reality must be face, but not uncritically. It is significant that we discover the idealization of the democratic city-state in classical Greek political thought, the endorsement of absolute monarchy in Hobbes, the deification of the Prussian state in Hegel, the eulogy of tribal mini-kingdoms in Ibn Khaldun and the sanctioning of the liberal-democratic state in the writings of the pluralists. If the societies we live in constrain us in the same way as gravity, there is still room for us to look beyond the horizon. A Muslim's faith is the shuttle he mounts to escape the confines of narrow realism.

## Modernity and the Muslim

It is fortunate that the reality of the modern nation-state and the international system within which it is embedded is not entirely hostile to Islamic ideals. Indeed, in some ways it has extended, and for the first time created, new possibilities for the advancement of these ideals. The conditions which exist today for the creation of truly global community serve the ideals of Islam which has announced itself as a global mission from its inception. The tendency towards democratization also represents a certain convergence with Islamic values. The techniques of popular representation and the development of mass communications offer, for the first time, the possibility of effecting the central concept of consensus, which is at the heart of Islamic doctrine. This concept can be operated even across the boundaries of national states, and thus help to achieve that cherished goal of a global Muslim community. The international movement towards greater freedom for individuals and groups to interact peacefully is also a fulfilment of the first demand the Prophet made on his tribe and the world around him: to be allowed to preach the divine message he received in peace and freedom. Muslims today, especially in the freer societies in the West, face fewer constraints on acting according to their Islamic faith than at most times in the past.

Nevertheless, the same modern developments have created a tension within Muslim communities and between them and the outside world. The concept of individual freedom which recognized no responsibility by the community for the spiritual welfare of the individual and only minimal concern for his or her material welfare is foreign to Islam. The Muslim community is under obligation to strive to attain the spiritual salvation of all its members, and that of the whole human race. This idea sometimes rules out the freedom of an individual to bring self-damnation, just as most modern societies outlaw suicide.

In the international sphere Muslims represent a global opposition force to the rising Western-inspired consensus which wants to remould the world in its own image. The international system confronts Muslims as an oppressive force at every level, limiting Muslim self-expression to a minimum. The most extreme example was, until recently, Bulgaria, where 'Muslim' names were outlawed. In neighbouring Yugoslavia, and in most other communist states until recently, Muslims face restrictions in education, worship and in such ritual acts as circumcision, which are forbidden. At another level, when Muslims are somewhat stronger and aspire to share in political power in their own countries, Muslim opponents may go to war to prevent their attaining power, as illustrated in Lebanon, Azerbaijan, Palestine and Kashmir. Finally, when Muslims achieve independence and sovereignty in their own lands and attempt to organize their lives according to their faith, they face ferocious international opposition, as has recently happened to Iran and Sudan.

However, this phase of crude repression is on its way out. In fighting oppression, Muslims find the liberal logic of the dominant order on their side. The real battle for the world has yet to begin: it will be fought in the moral and intellectual spheres. At one level Islam will have to become a major force in the international community, to achieve which it needs not only independence and force, but also moral strength. In tomorrow's world it will not be enough to be rich and to possess a mighty arsenal to make the Muslim voice heard. A powerful case is also required. For Islam the dilemma is to combine a commitment to peaceful interaction in the international arena with an equally strong commitment to justice and a mission to guide humankind to the right path.

The present international order is committed to grave injustices, from apartheid and Israeli aggression against Muslims and their lands to the unequal global distribution of wealth. The challenge to Islam is not only that it must convince the world that such injustices are incompatible with peaceful coexistence as long as they rest merely on brute force and have no moral justification or sanction from a globally recognized authority, but more significantly, Islam must redefine these causes in its own terms. Islam is not committed to the defence of the national rights of the Palestinians and black South Africans simply because the present international order has made them international issues. Nor can Islam discuss the global redistribution of wealth only to enhance the stability of the present international order and give it a face-lift, which could be a trap, especially since Muslims are interested parties in some cases. One cannot be a beggar at the door of the West and a judge on its actions simultaneously.

For a community that views itself as 'a witness over mankind', the issues must be radically redefined. Self-interest must be transcended in favour of global responsibility. The key is to reduce dependence on the outside world, not simply by attaining that elusive self-sufficiency, but by achieving self-reliance through renouncing claims over what others possess and use as weapons against Muslims. There is much that humanity can do without in the consumer madness that has engulfed us in modern times. Muslims are prisoners of the West precisely because, like their opponents, they have developed an insatiable appetite for luxuries. In our fast-depleted planet, Muslims can again offer an example by wanting less in a world where everyone is asking for more. Then they can offer an alternative to an international order based on the egotistic nation-state, which is in turn a collection of self-interested individuals and groups.

Muslims have also become dependent on the international system in another way. Because the modern Islamic revival was motivated primarily by a concern for the declining international prestige of  Muslims, modern Muslim activists have tended to use Islam to support their demands for an improvement in material living-standards and to advertise Islam as the best tool to achieve this goal.

This stance worked to the detriment of a cogent presentation of the Islamic message, for if the goal was the betterment of the worldly lot of the community, other approaches could arguably achieve it more quickly and at a lower cost. Counter-arguments are put forward in the theses of Qutb and Maududi regarding the global mission of Islam. However, these two great authors have written in a hegemonistic tone which accorded ill with their actual positions as leaders of tiny and marginalized groups of activists. These ideas should be recast in a moral context by redefining the role of the Muslim umma as the conscience of humankind.

## Redefining the Heritage

Much ink has been spilt on calls to redefine the Muslim intellectual and social heritage. Traditional political theory was a constant target, perhaps rightly so. Many modern commentators charge that the classical theory of the Caliphate is confused and idealistic, making it totally irrelevant for practical implementation in modern times. It must be remembered, however, that the classical theory was based on the concrete experience of the umma; this theory, therefore, does not reflect merely the ideal demands of faith, but a considered judgement on the history of the umma. A consensus has developed among Muslims to select the particular segment of Islamic history which came closest to realizing the ideals cherished by the Muslim umma. The Righteous Caliphate thus became a symbol for generations of Muslims. It inspired many successful attempts to revive the ideals it embodied, and to reaffirm them in practice. With each success, as happened during the rule of Omar ibn Abd al-Aziz (d. 101/720) or al-Zahir bi-Amrillah (d. 623\1325), new hope was generated for the transcendence of the reality towards the ideal, in spite of apparently insurmountable obstacles.

To understand the nature of the Muslim predicament, it is crucial to answer two important questions: (a) why was the ideal of the Righteous Caliphate so difficult to sustain and why did it elude Muslims for so long? and (b) what was wrong with the way Muslim thinkers understood and interpreted that ideal?

The two questions are related, for on closer analysis it seems that the inadequacy of the classical interpretation of the ideal was the basic reason why the ideal was allowed to collapse, and therefore why it became so difficult to revive it. Muslim thinkers pictured the ideal of the Righteous Caliphate as a mirage which they set the umma to chase until it was out of breath. And at the same time, these thinkers operated with two sets of contradictory assumptions. They seemed to believe in their hearts that this world was incorrigible, and that one would never again meet men such as Abu-Bakr or Omar, let alone the Prophet. Yet, they persisted in detailing a job description for a ruler who could only be a prophet or a saint. This attitude was bound to engender the cynicism of such men as Ibn Khaldun who, like Hobbes many centuries later, believed that men were self-interested brutes who could only be restrained by force, and that they deserved whatever they received from the tyrants needed to keep the peace among them. When faced by evidence contradicting their assumptions, such as the history of the Righteous Caliphate, these men argued that this was a miracle, an exception that proved the rule.

It is fortunate that in our time the ideas of Hobbes and others were refuted by experience. It has been proved practically possible to have in this very wicked world governments that are reasonably fair. This happened precisely by extending Hobbes's assumptions about the wickedness of men to include rulers and governments. By positing an in-built tendency in governments towards tyranny, it was possible to devise governments which would not allow rulers enough freedom to turn into tyrants, a quite successful arrangement. Thus, although former U.S. president Richard Nixon may have had the potential to be as tyrannical as Joseph Stalin, he was prevented from achieving this by a system which restricted his despotic tendencies.

A major flaw, therefore, in the traditional Muslim perception of the Righteous Caliphate was the erroneous belief that the rules of government must be designed to fit rulers who were almost saints--saints do not need the rules anyway. The rules laid down by Muslim theoreticians were derived from the actual practice of the saintly Righteous Caliphs, who were acting in the absence of any rules. Moreover, saintly men such as Omar ibn Abd al-Aziz acted virtuously and courageously in spite of the rules and conventions which in their time supported and encouraged corruption. Rules only become necessary when we are dealing with people who need guidance and restraint, which is the reason classical political theory was misguided and largely irrelevant to societies where saints were hard to find.

Another major problem with the classical theory was that it appeared to interpret the actions of the Righteous Caliphs in isolation. It failed, therefore, to explain why, when both Omar and Ali are accepted as Righteous Caliphs, the reign of the first was relatively tranquil and prosperous, while that of the latter was full of strife and turmoil. The way the whole community conducted themselves was crucial to the manner in which decisions were taken, accepted and implemented. It was therefore a grave error to describe early Muslim government in terms of the actions of one virtuous ruler, for that government consisted of a complex decision-making structure which classical theory failed to take into account. Had such essential features also been considered, one could have described the complete structure and conditions which made that virtuous government possible, which in turn would have enabled these conditions to be recreated under different circumstances. One obvious point would have been to note that the homogeneity of the early Medina community--the mutual trust between the leading figures in the community, the ease of communication between the different leaders (all resided in Medina or were otherwise in direct contact with the Caliph) and the charisma of the early caliphs--made it unnecessary to have a formal decision-making structure which allowed all leading figures to take part in the political process. In different circumstances where the leader lacked charisma or where communication was too cumbersome, more formal arrangements were needed. In fact, the very idea of having to have a single caliph or ruler may have to be scrapped in favour of a council or another body which would compensate for the shortcomings of individuals by pooling expertise and resources.

## The Nature of Modern Islamic Activism

While such confusion was not a particularly acute problem for earlier Muslim generations, it has become a serious handicap in the extremely complicated and radically different modern world. Now it has become more imperative than ever to strip the classical Muslim model to its essentials in order to recast classical theory.

This process has been embarked upon by successive Muslim generations since Sayyid Jamal ad-Din al-Afghani and his disciple Muhammad Abduh turned their attention to this issue in the last quarter of the nineteenth century. The exercise led to the dominance of freelance activism as the basis of Islamic reform, a situation further enhanced by the collapse of the caliphate and the rise of organized modern Islamic activism in the 1920s. It is not that the incidence of individual charismatic reformers in Islamic history was rare, given that the task of defining and outlining Islamic doctrine defied all formal institutionalization in the past. However, modern Islamic activism was radically different from conventional reformist/Mahdist movements in that it sought to attain this institutionalization. It aimed to redefine doctrine so as to restore authority on the basis of this redefined doctrine, as a remedy for the total collapse of traditional institutions and the doctrinal interpretations that underpinned them.

The emergence of this modern activism highlighted another area of confusion in traditional Muslim thought. Traditional theory defined public duties (such as the establishment of the state or the protection of the faith) as collective duties (*fard kifaya*), as opposed to individual duties (*fard ayn*). Fard kifaya was defined as that obligation which, if carried out by any group of Muslims, absolves all others from blame; but if it is not shouldered by anyone, it will lay all Muslims open to blame. This rendering created the impression that public duties did not concern individuals or the community as a whole unless they were neglected. The establishment of an Islamic state and its proper maintenance was thus not regarded as the responsibility of ordinary individuals. It was the collective duty of *ahl al-Hal wal-Aqd* (men of authority). And as long as any group of pretenders sustained the claim to being these men of authority, then the general public were lulled into perpetual passiveness.

It was only with the collapse of the khilafa early in the twentieth century that the Muslim conscience was shocked out of its slumbers, and Muslims suddenly realized that they were all in sin because no pretender of the khilafa existed. This was the basis on which the modern Islamist groups emerged and assumed the role of the umma's conscience. They are volunteers who decided to carry the banner left lying on the ground. But this eventuality points to the problem of the original concepts. It should never have been acceptable in the first place that the 'collective duty' be abandoned to no matter whom, without some positive input from the umma. A collective duty should be redefined to mean not that marginally important obligation from which everyone is absolved if anyone takes care of it. On the contrary, it should be the obligation of every individual in the community to see that this duty is carried out by the right person, no one being absolved until this was positively assured. The term fard kifaya should be changed to *fard jamai* (collective duty), for that is what it is.

The conditions for this redefinition have been created by modern constitutional practice, which has indicated how it is possible to build and supervise institutions for performing collective tasks. It has also given more power to the individual, whereas in the past, power in all societies rested with the nobility or other groups in authority. The new conditions which have emerged, through developments in communications and knowledge, have enabled many other groups to have a say in how things are operated. This in turn has increased the responsibility of each individual, since there is a sense in which every individual input counts. In Islam, as in matters of faith in general, this individual responsibility is the key to the system. God does not judge people by groups in the hereafter, but individually. In this sense the increase in individual efficacy should mean that everyone should be better able to discharge his or her religious duties, and must therefore shoulder more responsibility for putting communal life right.

Another major problem with the current Islamic revival is that it has chosen to be outward-oriented. The less-than-perfect traditional Islamic order has been sustained and tolerated only because of its outward successes. It shone like a lone star in a world of darkness and rampant injustice; it protected Muslims against encroachments of infidel barbarians. When the fire at the centre of the system appeared to be dying out, two contradictory responses emerged. On the one hand, confidence in the internal system was undermined. On the other, reformers tended to support

Muslim systems in spite of their corruption, for they saw in them the final line of defence against alien invading powers. Thus, we find reformers such as Afghani who, although critical of Muslim regimes, nevertheless agreed that any Muslim regime was better than an alien one. They were also prepared to compromise with non-Muslim inhabitants of Muslim lands to form a common front to defend the Muslim homeland against Western designs.

This attitude was reinforced by the experience of colonialism and the struggle against zionism and other anti-Muslim movements. Modern Muslim activists supported despotic and corrupt regimes in the Arab world or Pakistan so long as they took a belligerent anti-Israeli or anti-Indian stance, even though this attitude proved counterproductive. The Muslim world now contains some of the worst regimes on earth and it has made next to no progress in the battle against its enemies. In fact, it is precisely the nature of these regimes which led to this situation. Despotic regimes deprived of the confidence of their people have had to rely on the very enemies they were supposed to combat to keep them in power. Their appalling records also lent succour to those enemies by giving them the moral edge over Muslims, who are perpetually ashamed of their history.

There are several reasons for the predicament of modern Muslim societies which have attained neither the standards set by their faith, nor even been able to be as good as the infidels appeared to be. First, the age-old spirit of compromise and half-solutions survived and coloured the spirit of the modern Islamic revival. Now Islamists are divided among factions, each of which support a particular despotic regime. There are those who support Iranian despotism, those who prefer the Saudi variety and even those who like the Iraqi one. Conspicuously absent are those who reject and condemn all despotism on principle.

Second, Muslim activists have given priority to the fight against foreign enemies, and sacrificed the push for internal reforms for this end. All sorts of corruption, despotism, mismanagement and ineptitude was tolerated in the name of the fight against this enemy or that. The enemy within, that original sinner who sustained all other sins, was left undisturbed pending the elusive victory over the ever-multiplying foreign enemies. The most striking example of this was the Islamic revolution in Iran, which was all but aborted in the futile pursuit of real and imagined enemies, distracting attention from serious internal challenges that called for decisive solutions.

## *Totalitarianism and the Concept of Islamic Community*

An even more serious handicap is found in the adoption by today's Islamists of the modern concept of the state as a principle of restriction and control, without subscribing to the liberal and individualistic morality which underpins this concept. This misinterpretation has tended to make modern Islamists into proto-fascists, obsessed with dragging their compatriots kicking and screaming into paradise, which, of course, was not the original Islamic idea of a political community. The original Muslim community was united first by faith and mutual solidarity, and only secondarily by coercive power. Many modern Islamists seem to seek coercive power first and faith as its derivative.

A solution to this dilemma could be found in the proposals of the Tunisian Islamists, whose idea of democracy and freedom as the basis of any political association seems to provide a way out of the impasse in which Muslims are currently living. The problem of most, if not all, Muslim societies is that they do not have freedom to be anything. Concerned leaders of Muslim opinion in the past were worried that too much freedom would permit Muslims to drift away from Islam. This attitude pointed to a profoundly pessimistic streak in traditional Muslim thought, and proved to be generally mistaken. Unfortunately, it led the ulema to favour Islamically inclined despots over what seemed to them the rather uncertain outcome of 'chaos'. The same outlook was inherited by Islamists who were profoundly mistrustful of free popular will, which appeared to them inherently tending towards deviation from Islamic principles. They thus constantly sought comfort in some rather strict authoritarianism, which they hoped would keep people on the right path. The constant disappointments they have faced have yet to convince most of these groups that authoritarianism is more a source of corruption than freedom. The experience of today's Muslim societies where coercion is more frequently used to subvert than to promote Islamic ethics should be proof enough.

The search for an Islamic state must start with the search for freedom for Muslims. Freedom to think, to act, to sin, to repent and finally to find oneself and one's fulfilment in obeying God. Only then can the righteous Muslim community and its product, the virtuous Islamic state, emerge. For the present, then, the true Muslim's fight should be for one thing: democracy, the right of every individual not to be coerced into doing anything. In its freedom this society will find itself and develop its ethical standpoint, and then fashion the state after its own image and on the model of the prophetic community. In such a community, we know from history, men and women came voluntarily to submit themselves to the sanctions of the divinely ordained and sanctioned authority. Not only were they not hunted by the secret police, but they rejected offers to make use of the loopholes in the law to absolve themselves from punishment. It was their consciences that ruled them, not an impersonal or alien state. That was the ultimate freedom.

We must sound a note of caution here. Freedom does not necessarily imply lack of all constraints, including moral constraints. To be free does not mean to be amoral as is implied by certain interpretations of liberalism. Liberalism is, in fact, merely the rejection of a certain set of moral constraints in favour of another. Freedom implies lack of external undesirable constraints. We do not resent the restrictions on our personal freedoms posed by our moral principles or the need to care for our loved ones. However, some modern interpretations of the principle of freedom have led to disastrous consequences by neglecting this qualification. In the name of freeing men from the constraints 'imposed' by religion, all sorts of despots from Stalin to Atatürk and Suharto have headed repressive regimes of the most repulsive variety.

This warning must not be taken, however, to support the opposing claim, that an Islamic state must be totalitarian. Nothing is further from the truth. The Muslim community, and not an impersonal state, has a duty to afford each individual the maximum help in achieving his or her moral potential, which can be done by example, exhortation and by shielding the individual from undue pressures and temptations. However, the community cannot shoulder the individual's ultimate responsibility for his or her own actions, nor replace the individual's duty to prove his or her own moral worth and act as an example to others.

Muslims have erred in this direction. Some Muslims have equated the khalifa with God by giving him the right to force the community into acting against their consciences. This was the inevitable consequence of viewing the khalifa as a saint, and the community as impotent and sin-prone, a *raiyya* (herd) to be shepherded by its wise herdsman. The freedom denied to the herd was allowed to the shepherd, and shepherds have consistently turned out to be wolves.

### The State for the Muslims

To summarize with concrete suggestions on the shape of the Islamic state, we shall start by insisting that the basis for the re-establishment of the Muslim community (as a pre-condition for the setting-up of an Islamic state) must be the reaffirmation of the freedom and dignity of the individual Muslim. The ideal state for today's Muslim, or the ideal Islamic state at any time, should first and foremost be democratic. There is no need here to become involved with sterile disputes about terms, and the ill-advised circumlocutions about the Islamic state being a 'theo-democracy', or the relations between democracy and *shura* (consultation). Any state, whether Islamic or not, must be based on the free will of its citizens. A state formed by a Muslim community will by necessity be an Islamic state, one based on the sharia. It is inconceivable that in a Muslim community an argument should arise about following this or that command of God. The provisos set forth by extra-cautious theoreticians who insist that an Islamic state cannot be a democracy because that would imply that the will of the people is above all law, including sharia, is misplaced. If a community rejected sharia, it is by definition not Islamic, and the arguments of these writers are therefore irrelevant to it. Nevertheless, disputes within a Muslim community are bound to arise, as in the past, about many other things. However, democracy means that these differences should be resolved peacefully according to an agreed procedure, which is equitable and fair.

Democracy is therefore essential for any Muslim group whether it has attained the status of a true Islamic community or not. There is no point in saying, as did Maududi and Qutb, that we have no business prescribing for a community that has not accepted sharia. In a pre-sharia community the conditions for guiding society back to Islam can be supplied only by democracy, where the operation of the community and the demands of Islam are freely debated and refashioned. If society decides to make the transition to sharia, then democracy is needed to keep it together and resolve its differences.

An Islamic state should also be independent and self-reliant. It does not have to be aggressive and disruptive, but it should be firm in its moral convictions, and noble in its aversion to enslavement to the consumerism which has reduced most communities on our planets to grazing herds of mindless seekers after unhealthy comforts.

This state should be outward-looking, reasserting itself in the international arena and acting as a focus for the global community of Muslims. The unity it seeks should not be enforced, but it should seek to promote a shared outlook which asserts the collective view of Muslims on how the international order should function.

An ideal Muslim state should also be plural. It is not necessary for Muslims to allow the modern concept of territorial state sovereignty to imprison groups within a unitary scheme that stifles all diversity. A true pluralism is important for accommodating non-Muslims within an Islamic polity without either diluting it or relegating them to second-class citizenship, as well as for Muslims since we are fast approaching the emergence of a world community in which Muslims as a bloc are a minority. The rights of communities and individuals within this system must be defined to assure coexistence with the maximum freedom for all. It is a strong possibility that, as happened in the past, the exemplary behaviour of Muslims would in time convince their neighbours that theirs is the right path. In the meantime, an Islamic territory must be governed by a pluralistic polity of coexisting but independent communities, governed by treaties rather than by a constitution. The treaty should detail the rights and duties of each community for the safeguarding of common existence, in a similar way to that of the *sahifat al-Madina*. This could present an imaginative solution to a vexing problem.

Finally, an Islamic state must be a light for all humankind. It cannot be, like today's nation-states, engrossed in the endless search for unhealthy comforts and material goods for its citizens. Rather than being such an acquisitive black hole, the Islamic state should shine outwards and embody a philosophy of giving. There should not be 'interest-groups' vying with one another for what they can squeeze out of the system, but competition should be over how much can be given. What such a community can offer to the world is without limit.

6

# Conclusion

IF THE FOREGOING discussion has any validity, then one has to
infer that the concept of an Islamic state must be completely
abandoned if sanity is to return to Muslim political discourse. One should rather speak about a state for the
Muslims, or an Islamic political community. One must also
abandon the illusions about the millennium promised by the
revival of a utopian polity in which a righteous and saintly
ruler will miraculously emerge to restore the long-lost
golden age of Islam. Nor is it wise to shift our millennial
hopes to the newly emerged Islamic movements, and expect
that their accession to power will automatically bring an era
of divine justice and saintly rule. There is simply no
alternative to attaining these objectives the hard way, by
doing what is needed to achieve them.

Wisdom dictates that we should be pessimistic about the
qualities of our rulers, something which should not be too
difficult, given our experiences. The institutions of a
Muslim polity, and the rules devised to govern it, should
therefore be based on expecting the worst. Human experience shows that democracy, broadly defined, offers the best
possible method of avoiding such disappointment in rulers,
and affords a way of remedying the causes for such disappointments once they occur.

The value of this approach is that it does not make the

attainment of dignity and freedom of Muslim individuals contingent on the setting-up of a utopian Islamic state which we may never live to see. It also removes the grounds on which the current tyrannies ruling the Muslim world are justified. The tyrants lording it over the Muslims today, aided and abetted by their foreign allies, justify their existence by fear of Muslim 'fanatics' who want to coerce others into adopting an unacceptable lifestyle. This lame excuse for tyranny must be removed by affirming our commitment to democracy as the governing principle of the Muslim polity in all its stages. The state for Muslims must be a principle of liberation based on pluralism, with no coercion involved other than the minimum inherent in the principle of community itself.

The raison d'être of a political community is to assure the peaceful coexistence among its members. A Muslim political community is therefore an institution required to ensure that Muslims live in peace and harmony with one another, with other communities within the territory ruled by their polity and with other nations and communities on our planet. This peaceful co-existence has to be based on the rules of equity and fairness, and must not force Muslims to live contrary to their principles. The central misunderstanding of current Muslim political thought is the confused belief that a state based on Islamic principles is one which forces people to live according to Islam. In truth, the purpose of an Islamic political community is to enable individual Muslims to live according to Islam, and to protect them from coercion which tends to subvert their commitment to Islam. All the current references to the 'imposition of sharia' or the Islamic state, whether by Islamic thinkers or opponents of Islam, actually misunderstand the issue completely. Sharia can rule truly only when the community observing it perceives this as a liberating act, as the true fulfilment of the self and moral worth of the community and each individual within it, for sharia can never be imposed.

When it is imposed, it is not sharia. When only coercion underpins sharia, it becomes hypocrisy.

A Muslim polity must also defend the right of Muslims to live freely according to the dictates of their consciences, by force if necessary, for a Muslim state must use all its resources to fight injustice and tyranny inside and around it. We cannot expect the commitment to peace to be a licence for the toleration of all evils in the name of avoiding conflict. This was the central mistake of classical Muslim political theory, which has neither succeeded in avoiding conflict nor in achieving justice. Therefore, it is essential to strive for justice as the only firm basis for permanent peace and harmony.

To attain these goals, the Muslim state must rely primarily on the responsibility and active role of the individual within the community. It reasserts the value of the individual without preaching individualism. Classical Muslim political thought relegated the individual to the status of a non-entity by the postulation of vacuous and imprecise concepts such as that of ahl al-Hal wal-Aqd and fard kifaya. These confused notions provided the basis for the endorsement of practical secularism, or for making the legality of all Muslim social activity dependent on the will of a despot. It must be reaffirmed that the individual does not need the state to be a Muslim. He creates the state as a Muslim, and he creates it voluntarily to further enhance his Islamic life. The opinion given by al-Ghazali and others about the necessity of the state--any state--as the pre-condition of the legality of Muslim social life is the opposite of the truth. A despotic and illegal regime does not bestow legitimacy on subsidiary actions. On the contrary, it marks everything it touches with the stamp of illegality. For Muslims, to have no state at all is better than to have an illegal one.

It thus the responsibility of every Muslim individual to ensure that he or she organizes his or her communal life in accordance with Islam. The state, the Islamic party, the religious fraternity and the economic structure are all tools to achieve this end; Khomeini's assertion that the Islamic state is an end in itself loses all meaning if the state becomes unIslamic in the process of trying to guard and retain its Islamicity. Many Islamic parties and groups appear also to be fast losing their raison d'être by turning inwards and beginning to worship themselves instead of God. For them, the safeguard of their existence and status becomes a priority to which the bulk of Islamic moral principles is subordinated, even though they are not anywhere near to attaining state power.

All these are additional reasons why Muslims should be uncompromising in rejecting all Machiavellianism and justification of expedient shortcuts to our goals. Without lapsing into utopianism, Muslims must be wary of arguments like those used in the past to justify criminal acts in the name of necessity or higher ideals. It is important for every individual to realize that the only necessity constraining a person is that to which he or she voluntarily submits: necessity can justify imperfection, but never criminality. It might then be possible for Muslim individuals to live decent and dignified lives, and to escape imprisonment within sterile formulas that generated only confusion and suffering in the past.

To attain this end, the political ideals of the Muslims must be guided by the concept of the Muslim polity as a decentralized pluralistic association based primarily on choice rather than on coercion. The ideas I have outlined here suggest that the central ethical demands of Islam are less compatible with the modern concept of a coercive centralized state than with a free association of mutually co-operating communities. For such an organization the basis should be more like a treaty than a constitution. The origin of most modern constitutions was indeed a treaty. The English revolution of 1688 ended in a deal between the monarchy and nobility which laid down the rules for political conduct. The American constitution was also a kind of agreement between the influential members of the emerging community (the founding fathers or ahl al-Hal wal-Aqd) to regulate public life according to agreed principles. It was certainly different from the way the French revolution continued to attempt to impose a 'constitution' on the people some years later, an example faithfully followed by the Bolshevik and other revolutions. Unlike earlier attempts at regulating public life, the French and Bolshevik revolutions did not seek to implement the results of an emerging consensus, but wanted to impose on people what was perceived to be in their 'true' interest, even if the people 'out of ignorance or malice' did not agree.

Modern thinkers on the Muslim polity, led by Maududi who frankly applauded the Bolshevik model, reason along similar lines: since Islam is the ultimate truth, people must be ruled by it whether they like it or not. However, a second look at the Medina polity would call for a reassessment of this position. The Document of Medina (Sahifat al-Madina), hailed by modern Islamic scholars as the Medina Constitution, was in fact a treaty. The parties to that treaty included various tribes and clans in the Medina, among whom were several of the Jewish religion. The document laid down rules to be observed and responsibilities to be discharged for the maintenance and defence of the polity covering this broad coalition of communities.

The solution suggested by this model to the current dead-end path of the nation-state points to a new kind of polity, in which communities are joined together not as subjects to a sovereign all-powerful state, but as members of communities united voluntarily, each pursuing its own way of life in complete freedom. Of course, coercion is not ruled out entirely to safeguard and maintain the polity once it is established, but--and this is important--it is not the basis of the polity. A person should be able to join the community

and polity of her or his choice, and also to leave freely and join another. This element of choice is absent from the current international order, where most states insist that citizens conform to norms dictated from above, while freedom of movement to join another polity of one's choice is severely limited.

This lack of freedom is closely related to the territorial nature of the modern state. The model we are proposing here could suggest a way in which a polity is not strictly territorial. Political associations should make it possible for members to move in space without losing their rights of membership. This entails a concept of an international order based more on coexisting communities than on territorially-based mutually-exclusive nation-states. The European Community and the United States of America reflect some characteristics of the model we have in mind. Here, membership of a particular state does not preclude free movement between different states, nor is there a loss of any significant rights. A future international order based on Islamic principles would be comparable to these models. Various Muslim and non-Muslim communities would co-exist over an extensive area, and base this coexistence on mutually agreed treaties governing rights and duties towards the maintenance of the common polity. These rights and duties would not be affected by one's physical location, but by one's freely chosen commitment to the polity.

Such a polity will not be an intrusive, coercive organization seeking to impose specific norms and life-styles. It will, rather, be a co-operative association designed to help people live freely according to the dictates of their consciences. The key word here is 'treaty' as opposed to 'constitution', which is the regulating principle.

The polity would, of course, conform to sharia which is not 'imposed' but is the true expression of the free will of the community. With membership completely free, the Muslim community at the heart of this state is one that has chosen to live according to Islam and to obey sharia. This observance is essentially a matter of conscience, for sharia is truly observed only when people do so voluntarily and sincerely. Even the punishments for some public offences against the community or against oneself are not regarded as acts of social coercion but as exercises of purification and part of the social co-operation which preserves the worldly and spiritual health of the community.

To sum up, the central value governing the Islamic polity and giving it meaning is freedom. Even the ideal of social responsibility, which guards the Muslim community from drifting into individualism and disintegration, is based on complete freedom of conscience. A Muslim fulfils his or her social duty only if she or he does so voluntarily and without any coercion, even the coercion of social conformity.

# Notes

## *Chapter 1*

1. Harry Eckstein, 'On the "science" of the state', *Daedalus*, Fall (1979), p. 16.
2. Ibid., p. 17.
3. Ibn Khaldun's ideas were set forth in the *Muqaddimat* (introduction) to his work on history, first published in modern times in 1858 in two separate editions, one in Cairo edited by Nasr al-Hourini and the other in Paris edited by Etienne Quatremere. A three-volume English translation by Franz Rosenthal was published in 1958 (London: Routledge & Kegan Paul). Reference hereafter is to a later edition of the Arabic text (Beirut: Dar al-Fikr, n.d.).
4. Ibn Khaldun, op.cit., p. 34.
5. Ibid., pp. 150-1, 240-1.
6. Ibid., pp. 127-9.
7. Ibid., pp. 119-20.
8. Ibid., pp. 124-5.
9. See Machiavelli, *The Prince*....
10. Hobbes's ideas appeared mainly in his *Leviathan*.
11. Ibid., pp. 314-17, 322-4, 332-4.
12. Ibid., pp. 369ff.
13. D. Held, 'Central Perspectives on the Modern State', in McLennan, p. 41.

14. Tom Knox (ed.). *Hegel's Philosophy of Right.* London, 1967, p. 10.

15. Max Weber, 'Politics as a Vocation', in Gerth and Wright Mills, p. 78.

16. Hobbes, p. 161.

17. The expression is from the title of Macpherson's *Political Theory of Possessive Individualism.*

## Chapter 2

1. See Quran, 9:53-4, 83.

2. Quran 4:56.

3. See the text in Ibn Hisham's *al-Sirah al-Nabawiyyah.* Beirut: Dar Ihya al-Turath, n.d., vol. 2, pp. 147-50.

3. Quran 5:42.

5. See Jalal al-Din al-Suyuti, *Tarikh al-Khulafa.* Beirut: Dar al-Thaqafa, 1988, pp. 85ff.

6. Ibid., p. 24.

7. See al-Mawardi, p. 13.

8. Most of the writers cited as exponents of classical Muslim political theory are Shafi'is. These included al-Ghazali (d. 505/1111), al-Mawardi (d. 450/1058) and Ibn Jama'a (d. 733/1333).

## Chapter 3

1. See *al-Manar* **23** (1922), pp. 703ff.

2. An Arabic translation of Mustafa Kemal's speech was published in *al-Manar* **23**, pp. 772ff. Cf. Bernard Lewis, pp. 253ff.

3. See *al-Manar* **24** (1923), p. 283.

4. Ibid., **23**, pp. 712-3.

5. Ibid., pp. 784-5.

6. Ibid., p. 793.

7. Ibid., **24**, pp. 698ff.
8. For a good account of the controversy and a reproduction of the documents concerned, see Amara. Cf. al-Rayyis.
9. See Amara, pp. 27-8.
10. See Mahmoud Abd al-Halim, *al-Ikhwan al-Muslimoon, Ahdath Sana' at al-Tarikh,* Cairo, 1979, vol. I.
11. al-Banna, p. 74.
12. Ibid, pp. 78-81.
13. Ibid., especially pp. 162ff, 357ff.
14. See Qutb, *Ma'alim fi'l-Tariq.*
15. See Maududi, 'The Political Theory of Islam', in Ahmad. See also Maududi, *Islamic Law...,* and *Minhaj.*
16. See Hassan Turabi, *Tajdid al-Fikr al-Islami,* Khartoum, 1982; *Qadaya l ..;* and *al-Muslim bayna....*
17. See my profile on Sheikh Rashid al-Ghanoushi in *Inquiry,* October 1987, pp. 50-6.
18. See Khomeini.
19. See *Inquiry,* March 1988, pp. 18-20. Cf Arjomand, pp. 182-3.

## Chapter 4

1. Hobbes, *Leviathan,* pp. 187-8.
2. Cf. Niazi Berkes, *The Development of Secularism in Turkey,* Montreal, 1964, pp. 451-2; Lewis, pp. 252ff.
3. Lenin.
4. See Ernest Mandel, *Late Capitalism,* London: SNLB/Verso, 1975.
5. See, for example, Amin.
6. See *al-Madina,* 17 February 1990.
7. See Piscatori, pp. 42-3.
8. Ibid., p. 42.
9. Quran 31:14-15.
10. See al-Banna, *Rasail,* pp. 78ff, 102ff. Cf. Turabi, 'al-Sahwa al-Islamiyya wal-Dawla al-Qutriyya fil-Watan al-Arabi', paper read at Amman conference, October 1987.

11. See al-Faruqi's introduction to Abu Sulayman. For Turabi's ideas, see the pamphlet *Ilaqat al-Sudan wal-Siyassa al-Kharijiyya* (Sudanese Relations and Foreign Policy), produced by the National Islamic Front, Khartoum, 1988.

12. Maududi, *al-Jihad*...; and Qutb, *Maalim*..., pp. 55ff.

13. Ghanoushi, personal communication.

14. See Khadduri, 'The Islamic Theory of International Relations', in Proctor.

15. See, for example, the preface to Mitchell; and Kerr, *Islamic Reform*.

# Selected Bibliography

Abd al-Raziq, Ali. *al-Islam wa usul al-Hukm*. Cairo: Matbaat Misr, 1925.

Abu Sulayman, A. *The Islamic Theory of International Relations*. Herndon, Va.,: International Institute of Islamic Thought, 1987.

Ahmad, Khurshid (ed.). *Islam: Its Meaning and Message*. London: Islamic Council of Europe, 1976.

_____ and Zafar Ishaq Ansari. *Islamic Perspectives: Studies in Honour of Sayyid Abu Al Ala al-Mawdudi*. Leicester: Islamic Foundation, 1979.

Algar, Hamid. *Islam and Revolution: Writings and Declarations of Imam Khomeini*. Berkeley: Mizan Press, 1981.

Amara, M. *Marikat al-Islam wa Usul al-Hukm*. Cairo: Dar al-Shoruk, 1989.

Amin, Samir, et al. *Dynamics of Global Crisis*. New York: Monthly Review Press, 1982.

Arjomand, S.A. *The Turban for the Crown: The Islamic Revolution in Iran*. New York: Oxford University Press, 1988.

Ayoob, Mohammed (ed.). *The Politics of Islamic Reassertion*. London: Croom Helm, 1981.

al-Banna, Hasan. *Majmuat Rasail al-Imam al-Shahid Hasan al-Banna*. Beirut: Dar al-Qalam, 1974(?). English translation of selections by Charles Wendell. Berkeley: University of California Press, 1978.

_____. *Mudhakkirat al-Dawa wal-Daiya*. Cairo: al-Maktab al-Islami, 1983.

Cudsi, A.S. and Ali E. Hilali Dessouki. *Islam and Power*. London: Croom Helm, 1981.

Dahl, R. *Polyarchy*. New Haven: Yale University Press, 1971.

Dessouki, Ali E. Hilali (ed.). *Islamic Resurgence in the Arab World*. New York: Praeger, 1982.

Donohue, John and John Esposito. *Islam in Transition: Muslim Perspectives*. Oxford: Oxford University Press, 1982.

Dunleavy, P. and B. O'Leary. *Theories of the State*. London: Macmillan, 1987.

Dunn, J. *The Political Thought of John Locke*. Cambridge: Cambridge University Press, 1969.

Enayat, Hamid. *Modern Islamic Political Thought*. London: Macmillan, 1982.

Esposito, John. *Islam and Development: Religion and Socio-political Change*. Syracuse: Syracuse University Press, 1980.

_____. *Voices of Resurgent Islam*. New York: Oxford University Press, 1983.

_____. *Islam and Politics.* Syracuse: Syracuse University Press, 1984.

Fazlur Rahman. *Islam.* New York: Holt, Rinehart and Winston, 1966.

Gerth, H.H. and C. Wright Mills. *From Max Weber.* London: Routledge and Kegan Paul, 1970.

Ghanoushi, Rashid. *Maqalat.* Paris: Tunisian Islamic Trend Movement, 1984.

Gibb, H.A.R. *Modern Trends in Islam.* New York: Octagon Press, 1947.

Halpern, Manfred. *The Politics of Social Change in the Middle East and North Africa.*, Princeton: Princeton University Press, 1963.

Hamidullah, M. *Majmuat al-Wathaiq al-Siyasiyya lil-Ahd al-Nabawi wal-Khilafa al-Rashida.* Beirut: Dar al-Irshad, 1959.

Hobbes, T. *Leviathan* (edited by C.B. Macpherson). Harmondsworth: Penguin, 1968 (first published 1651).

Hosaini, Ishak Musa. *The Muslim Brethren: the Greatest Modern Islamic Movement.* Beirut: Khayat, 1956.

Hourani, Albert. *Arabic Thought in the Liberal Age.* Cambridge: CUP, 1983 (first published 1962).

Ibn Khaldun. *Muqaddimat Ibn Khaldun.* Beirut: Dar al-Fikr, n.d. English translation, Franz Rosenthal. London: Routledge & Kegan Paul, 1958.

Keddie, Nikki. *An Islamic Response to Imperialism: Political and Religious Writings of Sayyid Jamal ad-Din 'al-Afghani'.* Berkeley: University of California Press, 1968.

Kerr, Malcolm. *Islamic Reform: the Political and Legal Theories of Muhammad Abduh and Rashid Rida.* Berkeley: University of California Press, 1966.

Khalid, Kh.M. *al-Dawla fil-Islam.* Cairo: Dar al-Thabit, 1981.

Khomeini, Ayatollah Ruhollah. *al-Hukuma al-Islamiyya.* Tehran: Wazarat al-Irshad, n.d. (first published in 1971).

Kurdi, A.A. *The Islamic State.* London: Mansell, 1984.

Lenin, V.I. *Imperialism: the Highest Form of Capitalism.* Moscow: Progress Publishers, 1966.

Machiavelli, Niccolo. *The Prince and Other Political Writings* (translated and edited by Bruce Penman). London: Everyman's Library, 1981.

McLennan, G., et al (eds.). *The Idea of the Modern State.* Milton Keynes: Open University Press, 1984.

Macpherson, C.B. *The Political Theory of Possessive Individualism.* Oxford: OUP, 1963.

Maududi, Sayyid Abul Ala. *Islamic Law and Constitution.* Lahore: 1969.

_____. *Minhaj al-Inqilab al-Islami.* Beirut, 1979.

_____, et al. *al-Jihad fi Sabilillah.* Beirut: IIFSO, 1978.

al-Mawardi. *al-Ahkam al-Sultaniyya*. Cairo: Maktabat Mustafa al-Babi al-Halabi wa Awladuhu, 1966.

Mitchell, Richard P. *The Society of the Muslim Brothers*. London: Oxford University Press, 1969.

Nettl, J.P. 'The State as a Conceptual Variable', *World Politics* **XX** (1968), pp. 559-92.

Piscatori, James. *Islam in a World of Nation-States*. Cambridge: CUP, 1986.

_____ (ed.). *Islam in the Political Process*. Cambridge: CUP, 1983.

Proctor, J.H. *Islam and International Relations*. London: Pall Mall Press, 1965.

Qutb, Sayyid . *al-Adala al-Ijtimaiyya fil-Islam*. Beirut(?): Dar al-Katib al-Arabi, 1949.

_____. *Maalim fil-Taric*. Beirut: IIFSO, 1978.

Rawls, J. *A Theory of Justice*. Oxford: OUP, 1972.

al-Rayyis, M. Diyaddin. *al-Islam wal-Khilafa fil-Asr al-Hadith*. Beirut: Manshurat al-Asr al-Hadith, 1973.

Rodinson, Maxime. *Islam and Capitalism*. Harmondsworth: Penguin, 1974.

Said, Edward. *Orientalism*. New York: Vintage Books, 1979.

Smith, Wilfred Cantwell. *Modern Islam in India*. London: Gollancz, 1946.

_____. *Islam in Modern History.* Princeton: Princeton University Press, 1957.

Tibi, Bassam. *The Crisis of Modern Islam.* Salt Lake City: University of Utah Press, 1988.

Tilly, C.H. *The Formation of National States in Western Europe.* Princeton: Princeton University Press, 1975.

Turabi, Hassan. *Qadaya al-Hurriyya wal-Wahda.* Khartoum: Khartoum University Students Union, 1982.

_____. 'The Islamic State'. In Esposito, *Voices of Resurgent Islam,* 1983, pp. 241-51.

_____. *al-Haraka al-Islamiyya fil-Sudan.* Khartoum: Institute of Research and Social Studies, 1991.

_____. *al-Muslim Bayn al-Wujdan wal-Sultan.* London: Dar al-Sahwe, n.d.

Turner, Bryan S. *Weber and Islam.* London: Routledge & Kegan Paul, 1974.

Vatikiotis, P.J. *Islam and the State.* London: Croom Helm, 1987.

Voll, John Obert. *Islam: Continuity and Change in the Modern World.* Boulder: Westview Press, 1982.

# Index

Copyedited by Sylvia J. Hunt

Typography by Little Red Cloud

Cover design by Frances Ross

Composed in 11/12 pt English Times

Printed and bound by The Guernsey Press
of Vale, Guernsey, Channel Islands
on Munken 80gsm wood-free paper

# CHRISTIAN-MUSLIM RELATIONS
Yesterday, Today, Tomorrow

*Munawar A. Anees, Syed Z. Abedin & Ziauddin Sardar*

The death of communism removed the greatest insecurity of the West, but that fear and hatred is rapidly transferring to Islam. Much of the world is aligning itself with the Christian 'right' against the Muslim hordes, or with the Muslim 'right' against the infidels. It is time to stop this dissension and disorder.

In 'The Dialogue of History', Dr Anees surveys the history of relations between Islam and Christianity, which began propitiously when Muhammad advised a group of Muslims to seek refuge with the Christian King Negus of Abyssinia. In 'Believers and Promotion of Mutual Trust', Dr Abedin reasons that, given the mission orientation of both religions, theological distinctions should be put aside so that people of both faiths can come together to promote trust and community. In 'The Postmodern Age' when secularism has all but failed, Dr Sardar places the onus on Christians and Muslims to fill the emerging moral and social vacuum with an ethical system that is both distinctively contemporary and deeply rooted in authentic religious tradition.

Munawar A. Anees lectures at Mara Institute of Technology, Malaysia. Syed Z. Abedin is director of the Institute of Muslim Minority Affairs, Saudi Arabia. Ziauddin Sardar is an independent writer and journalist.

Religion. Christianity. Islam.

1991 112pp Paper 20x13cm ISBN 1-85640-021-2

# HOW WE KNOW
Ilm and the Revival of Knowledge

Edited by *Ziauddin Sardar*

In the flourishing classical Muslim civilization, Islam was synonymous with knowledge (ilm). Contemporary Muslim civilization, however, is like a stagnant lake, slowly but surely acidifying. The oxygen that can breathe fresh life into it is a fully-fledged revival of ilm. The pursuit, the generation, the processing, the retrieval, the dissemination, the analysis and the criticism of knowledge must become the prime focus of all Muslims and their societies. Once again, Islam must become, and be clearly seen to be, synonymous with knowledge.

In *How We Know*, four Muslim scholars dissect the problem:

What has happened to ilm since the classical period?
What has been the effect of imperialism?
Is there a way to revive the civilization of the book?
How do we learn Islamically?

They set down plans for re-educating Muslims so that all of them might recover the true meaning of knowledge for their own lives.

Munawar Anees lectures at Mara Institute of Technology, Malaysia. S. Parvez Manzoor is professor of linguistics at Stockholm University. Ibraheem Sulaiman is director of the Centre of Islamic Legal Studies, Nigeria. Ziauddin Sardar is a scholarly writer and futurist.

Education. Philosophy. Islam.

1991 160pp Paper 20x13cm ISBN 1-85640-020-4

# SCIENCE AND MUSLIM SOCIETIES

*Nasim Butt*

This is the first book to show clearly why science is important to modern Muslim societies and how the teaching of science can profit from the incorporation of an Islamic perspective.  The author

*      Explains why the Islamic holistic ethic can benefit both Muslim and non-Muslim.
*      Highlights the differences between Western and Islamic science, using examples of Islamic science in operation.
*      Identifies new developments, such as those in medicine and bio-technology, where value-judgements must be made and where for Muslims an Islamic scientific input is essential.
*      Demonstrates how the educational issues that constantly crop up in modern science education may be dealt with Islamically.

In conclusion, the author discusses and illustrates how science in the classroom may be humanized and how religion may be integrated into the science curriculum.

Nasim Butt is Head of Science, King Fahad Academy, London, and Educational Consultant to the Iqra Trust.

Science education. Islam.

1991  144pp  paper  20x13cm  ISBN 1-85640-023-9

# Other GREY SEAL titles

*Distorted Imagination: Lessons from the Rushdie Affair* by Merryl Wyn Davies and Ziauddin Sardar. Traces the 1,000-year history of the Rushdie affair, explains its emotionally-charged present and predicts its devastatingly long future. 'A carefully argued book which [everyone] who wants a multi-cultural, multi-ethnic society must read' *Day by Day*.

1990 312pp Hb 24x16cm ISBN-1-85640-000-X

*Khomeini's Forgotten Sons: The Story of Iran's Boy Soldiers* by Ian Brown. A tale of conflict and suffering and the brutalization of children who were forced into war at eleven, twelve or thirteen. 'A valuable story of ordinary young people caught up in a murderous Middle Eastern war machine' The Tablet.

1990 208pp Hb 22x14cm ISBN-1085640-002-6

*Israel's Nuclear Weaponry: A New Arm's Race in the Middle East* by Honoré M. Catudal, Jr. Reveals how and why Israel acquired nuclear weapons, her nuclear delivery potential and Arab reaction. This 'fascinating book, full of drama...is essential reading for all those interested in international affairs' *Conflict Bulletin*.

1991 152pp Hb 22x14cm ISBN-1-85640-019-0

*Turabi's Revolution: Islam and Power in Sudan* by Abdelwahab El-Affendi. Places Sudan's current affairs in the context of the Islamic revivalist tide and demonstrates how other Islamic countries might benefit from the Sudanese experience. 'Compulsory reading for all Muslims' *Africa Events*.

1991 226pp Hb 24x16cm ISBN-1-85640-004-2

*The Light in the Enlightenment: Christianity and the Secular Heritage* by Shabbir Akhtar. A forceful defence of Christianity against indifference, atheism and the politically expedient religious pluralism of the secular world. 'Lucid, well-informed and closely argued' (Bishop Lesslie Newbigin).

1990 224pp Hb 22x14cm ISBN 1-85640-001-8